Welcome to the Church Year

An Introduction
to the Seasons
of the Episcopal Church

Vicki K. Black

MOREHOUSE PUBLISHING
A Continuum imprint
HARRISBURG • LONDON • NEW YORK

Morehouse Publishing
P.O. Box 1321
Harrisburg, PA 17105

Morehouse Publishing is a Continuum imprint.

Design by Corey Kent

Library of Congress Cataloging-in-Publication Data

Black, Vicki K.
  Welcome to the church year: an introduction to the seasons of the Episcopal church / Vicki K. Black.
    p. cm.
  ISBN 0-8192-1966-5 (pbk.)
  1. Church year. I. Title.
  BV30.B54 2004
  263'.9—dc22   2003026719

Printed in the United States of America

04 05 06 07 08 09   6 5 4 3 2 1

Welcome to the Church Year

For Benjamin and John

Contents

1   Welcome to the Church Year 1
     What Is the Church Year?   2
     Time in the Church Year   3
     The Two Cycles of the Church Year   5
     The Development of the Liturgical Calendar   6
     The Lectionary   9
     Traditions of the Christian Year   10
     Questions for Further Thought and Discussion   13

2   Advent 15
     Advent Themes   15
     Advent Traditions   17
          The Advent Wreath   17
          The Advent Calendar   19
          St. Nicholas   19
          Advent Lessons and Carols   20
     The Sunday Liturgy in Advent   21
          The Lectionary   22
          The Blessings   25
     Questions for Further Thought and Discussion   26

3   Christmas 27
     Christmas Themes   28
     Christmas Services   31
          The Lectionary   32
     The Twelve Days of Christmas   34
          The Holy Name   35
          Christmas Lessons and Carols   36
     Questions for Further Thought and Discussion   38

4   The Epiphany 39
    Epiphany Themes   40
    The Feast of the Epiphany   41
    The Baptism of Our Lord   43
    The Sundays after the Epiphany   44
    Holy Days in Epiphany   46
    Epiphany Blessings   47
    Questions for Further Thought and Discussion   49

5   Lent 51
    Lenten Themes   53
    Lenten Traditions   55
        Spiritual Disciplines   56
        The Way of the Cross   57
    Ash Wednesday   57
    The Sunday Liturgy in Lent   60
        The Penitential Order   61
        The Great Litany   62
        The Catechumenate   63
        The Lectionary   63
        The Prayer over the People   64
    The Weekdays of Lent   65
    Questions for Further Thought and Discussion   66

6   Holy Week 67
    Holy Week in the Early Church   68
    Holy Week in the Episcopal Church Today   71
    Palm Sunday   73
        The Liturgy of the Palms   74
        The Sunday of the Passion   75
    Monday, Tuesday, and Wednesday in Holy Week   77
        Tenebrae   78
    Maundy Thursday   79
        The Lessons   80
        The Footwashing   83
        The Reserved Sacrament   85

The Lord's Supper   86
The Stripping of the Altar   86
The Night Vigil   87
Good Friday   88
The Lessons   89
The Solemn Collects   90
The Veneration of the Cross   91
Communion from the Reserved Sacrament   92
Holy Saturday   93
Questions for Further Thought and Discussion   94

7   Easter to Pentecost 95
Easter Themes   97
Easter Traditions   99
The Easter Vigil   100
The Service of Light   101
The Service of Lessons   103
Christian Initiation   103
The Holy Eucharist   103
Easter Day   104
Easter Week and the Great Fifty Days   104
The Sunday Liturgy in Easter   106
The Ascension   107
The Day of Pentecost   109
Questions for Further Thought and Discussion   112

8   The Season after Pentecost 113
Trinity Sunday   114
Themes in the Season after Pentecost   118
Holy Days   120
The Transfiguration   121
All Saints' Day   122
The Last Sunday after Pentecost   123
Questions for Further Thought and Discussion   126

Notes 127

Welcome to the Church Year

When our son Benjamin was about four years old, he was given a Spirograph set at a birthday party. I was delighted to know they still made Spirographs after all these years. I still remember the hours I spent as a child, pen clutched tightly in hand, tracing the swirls and ellipses and spirals made with the various sets of plastic wheels turning around and around inside other wheels. Now Benjamin, too, is watching the amazing patterns that emerge as he circles the wheels over and over on the paper. The key is the number of repetitions: the more times he goes round the wheel, the more intricate and three-dimensional the picture he creates.

The same is true of the church year. Every year we cycle through the seasons from Advent through the Season after Pentecost, and with every repetition their meaning becomes more textured—richer, deeper, more subtle and complex. Sometimes a particular season will stand out for us in a given year and its message will take on fresh significance, while we will speed through another almost without noticing its passing. The repetition is the key to their gift of grace in our lives. Like the Spirograph's layers of single ellipses combining to form intricate spirals, the cycle of the repeating and overlapping cycles of the feasts and fasts of the church year create patterns of meaning in our lives, giving shape and direction to the events that mark our days.

Repeating the cycle of the seasons makes us aware of the passing of time. Most of us have had this experience with family holidays, or occasions such as high school or college reunions. As we decorate the Christmas tree or open gifts, we notice how our children have grown; as we gather around the Thanksgiving table, we are aware that our aging parents or grandparents—and we ourselves—have changed during the previous year.

We are also reminded of who we are, as we gather with family and friends and mark traditions that are part of our identity within the larger community. If the year has had difficult moments, we are perhaps a bit wiser and more sober than the year before, and also more aware of our dependence on God's merciful grace. If the year has been filled with joyful occasions and gifts of new life, we may find gratitude welling up as we sing familiar songs or tell a family story. For Christians, keeping the church year likewise becomes a means of grace in our lives: the repetition of the cycle of feasts and fasts teaches us who we are as followers of Christ and beloved children of God.

WHAT IS THE CHURCH YEAR?

While I was writing this book, whenever I told someone it was about the church year, the most common response would be a polite look of confusion and the embarrassed question, "Now, umm, what exactly *is* the church year?" The church year goes by any number of names—the Christian calendar, the liturgical year, the church's feasts and fasts, the seasons of the church—but it is essentially the cycle of days and seasons that mark occasions of special devotion in the Christian faith. The Book of Common Prayer officially calls this cycle of feasts and fasts "The Calendar of the Church Year." You can find a brief description and a list of the days in that section of the prayer book.[1]

Every culture, every religious tradition has its cycle of seasons, holy days (or holidays), and occasions of special commemoration. We know the earth's seasons of winter, spring, summer, and fall.

In the United States, for example, people celebrate national holidays such as Independence Day and Memorial Day. The calendar of the Christian year marks the occasions that have to do with the life of Jesus: his conception, birth, baptism, teaching, ministry, suffering, death, resurrection, and ascension. Someone has said that the church year "is the life of Christ lived out again in liturgical time—in the time and in the memory of his Church."[2] Other days in the church year focus on the church community, such as the coming of the Holy Spirit at Pentecost or the communion of believers throughout all time at All Saints' Day.

There are significant variations in the liturgical calendars of different traditions within the wider church, especially the Orthodox, Roman Catholic, Anglican, and Lutheran, though the broad outline of seasons is quite similar because all the calendars share common roots in the early church. The Orthodox dates for Christmas and Easter differ from those in the western churches, for example, because we have long followed different calendars. In this book, however, we will be focusing on the liturgical year as practiced in the Episcopal Church.

TIME IN THE CHURCH YEAR

Fundamental to the Christian year is the concept of time. Time can be measured in any number of ways: we order our days by using a common standard for minutes, hours, days, months, and years. Historians speak of time in terms of eras, geologists in terms of epochs or ages. We speak of meeting someone at noon or four P.M., and we also speak more generally of "a time" in our lives when we were students or newlyweds or first-time parents or recently retired. In the church year we likewise have two different approaches to time, and as we move through the seasons, we tend to blend them in our worship, prayer, and reflection.

The most straightforward approach to time in the church year is the historical approach, which the liturgical professor Marianne Micks once called a "tourist's view of time."[3] It became more prevalent during the fourth century, as churches in the Holy Land developed liturgies to mark the days of Holy Week and Easter at the various sites at which Jesus suffered, died, and rose again. Pilgrims began to travel to Jerusalem to participate in these liturgies, and they brought them back to other countries as they returned. We have the diary of one such pilgrim, Egeria, who visited Jerusalem in the year 385. She describes in great detail how the Jerusalem church marked the days of Lent, Holy Week, and Easter with a series of liturgies that recalled the historical events at the end of Jesus' ministry.

In the historical approach to the church year we, too, like the pilgrims in Jerusalem, follow the life of Jesus step by step, from his conception and birth through his baptism and years of ministry and teaching to his suffering, death, resurrection, and ascension. As Micks puts it, "The historical approach offers a chance to relive in microcosm every twelve months what Jesus himself experienced in his thirty-some years. By walking in his footsteps one imitates his rhythms."[4]

The second approach to time in the church year is one that actually predates the historical perspective, and might be described with words like mystical, theological, or eschatological (meaning the end of all time, or outside time as we know it). It is a way to understand and participate in the eternal and mysterious meaning of the holy days of the calendar, beyond all time and human history. In Micks's words, what she calls the "mystery" approach

> offers Christians a chance instead to experience the full mystery of God's plan for mankind, not only in each Eucharist but also in each full cycle of Christian holidays. The stress in this interpretation is on times and seasons wherein Christian worshipers encounter the power of the Holy Spirit to make present that which has already happened and which is yet to come.[5]

The liturgical scholar Massey Shepherd echoes this theme when he writes, "The Christian year is a mystery through which every moment and all times and seasons of this life are transcended and fulfilled in that reality which is beyond time."[6]

As you move through the seasons of the church year in the Epis-copal Church today, you will probably see both of these approaches to time in the services you attend. At Christmas, for example, you will hear the story of Mary and Joseph traveling to Bethlehem and of Jesus' birth there. At the Christmas pageant you may see the visits of shepherds and wise men and angels. At the same time, you will also hear words like "Incarnation" and "Logos" and "Word-made-flesh"—theological words the church uses to talk, however dimly, about its ongoing experience of Jesus, fully God and fully man, who lived among us and who lives among us still. In historical time, Christmas happened over two thousand years ago in Bethlehem; in theological time, Christmas happens now, in the mystery of God choosing to dwell within humankind, a mystery that transcends all time.

THE TWO CYCLES OF THE CHURCH YEAR

There are two main patterns for the seasons in the church year: the Lent-Easter-Pentecost cycle and the Advent-Christmas-Epiphany cycle. In the weeks not included in these seasons, we do not have real "seasons" but "Sundays After": the Sundays after the Epiphany and the Sundays after Pentecost. During these weeks the Sunday celebration of the resurrection is the primary focus.

The dates for Lent, Holy Week, and Easter move around each year according to the date of Easter, which is determined each year by the date of the first full moon after March 21. Easter thus is set by the lunar calendar. This is the calendar that the Jews used at the time of Jesus to determine the date of Passover, and the one Christians continued to use in the days of the early church. The cycle for Advent, Christmas, and Epiphany, on the other hand, is set by the fixed date of December 25: the first Sunday of Advent is always four Sundays before Christmas Day. This cycle is set by the solar calendar used in the Roman Empire; it is the one we are most familiar with today.

Within each season of the liturgical year are feast and fast days marking events in Jesus' life, in particular saints' lives, or for special occasions. Some celebrations are called "Principal Feasts" because they take precedence over any other holy day when there is over-lap: these are Easter Day, Ascension Day, the Day of Pentecost, Trinity Sunday, All Saints' Day, Christmas Day, and the Epiphany. Other holy days are identified as "major" or "minor," based on the closeness of their association with Jesus' life, death, and resurrection, and their basis in Scripture. You will sometimes hear the major feasts called "red-letter days," from the old custom of printing church calendars in two colors: red for major feasts and black for lesser feasts. Today, people still refer to important days in their lives as "red-letter days."

A major feast, for example, is the Annunciation—March 25, the day we mark the appearance of the angel to Mary announcing the coming birth of Jesus. The minor (or lesser) feast days include commemorations of the saints throughout the ages, such as Julian of Norwich on May 8 or the Martyrs of Uganda on June 3. When major or minor feasts happen to fall on a Sunday, however, the Sunday celebration of the Eucharist always takes precedence. When March 17 falls on a Sunday, for example, we always celebrate the liturgy for a Sunday in Lent rather than the feast day for St. Patrick.

When you attend a service in an Episcopal church, you can usually determine which season or feast day is being celebrated that day by checking the service leaflet or bulletin. It will indicate which Sunday within the season that particular day marks (such as "The Sixth Sunday of Easter") or the name of the feast being celebrated (such as "All Saints' Day"). You can also gather clues by the color of the vestments and altar hangings (white for Easter, green for the Season after Pentecost, and so on), by the theme of the gospel lesson that is read that day, and by the hymns that are chosen.

THE DEVELOPMENT OF THE LITURGICAL CALENDAR

The Christian year has its origins in the liturgical observances of Judaism, particularly as they were practiced around the time of Jesus. The basic unit of time for Jews then was the seven-day week, with a regular pattern of daily prayer and the keeping of the Sabbath. Jews gathered daily at the Temple in Jerusalem for ritual sacrifices and prayer, and weekly for Sabbath services in their synagogues to hear the Scriptures read and interpreted. Christians continued that pattern of daily and weekly prayer. From the beginning, they structured their week around Sunday, which they called "the Lord's Day," set apart as the day not only of Jesus' resurrection but also the day of the outpouring of the Holy Spirit. In the Jewish calendar, Sunday was known as the first day of the week, or sometimes the Eighth Day, symbolizing the fulfillment of time, the New Age. It was the day of creation, the day of light, and Christians adopted this day, rather than Saturday, the Jewish Sabbath, as their primary occasion of celebration.

Very early in the church's history, Christians began gathering every Sunday to celebrate the Eucharist, a ritual meal of bread and wine in which the presence of the risen Christ was revealed to them in the breaking of the bread and sharing of the cup. The Sunday Eucharist was thus the earliest feast of the church. Paul's first letter to the church in Corinth, written around the middle of the first century, tells us that Christians were gathering to keep the Lord's Supper soon after Jesus' death, resurrection, and ascension (1 Corinthians 11:23–26). Early church documents testify that attendance at this weekly gathering of disciples was seen as vital: "To abstain from this meal is to separate oneself from the Lord: the Sunday meal is that which we take in common with the Lord and with the brethren."[7] This practice of sharing in the Sunday Eucharist with other Christians was what identified someone as a Christian.

Sunday was thus the principal celebration of the early church, marking, week after week, the resurrection of the Lord. Soon, however, Christians began to celebrate other important events in the life of Jesus, and the church calendar of feasts and seasons emerged. The Christian educator Joseph P. Russell has called the church year "the first curriculum of the church," a way of teaching the faith to those who were preparing for baptism and who were being formed in the Christian tradition. He notes:

The familiar pattern of Advent/Christmas/Epiphany and Lent/ Holy Week/Easter evolved out of the need of the early church to guide candidates for baptism through the essential narratives and teachings that would form their understanding of God in Christ over the rest of their lives.[8]

The liturgical historian Marion J. Hatchett concurs: "The greatest influence on the development of the Christian year . . . was the liturgy of Christian initiation."[9] Baptism was the water rite that initiated someone into the church as a new Christian, or "little Christ," and the traditions and practices surrounding baptism were the kernel around which all other aspects of the church year developed. From the rites associated with Easter, baptisms developed the Great Fifty Days of Easter and the season we call Lent. Over time the fasting, study, prayers, and liturgies that early Christians used to prepare for and celebrate Easter became part of the fixed cycle of the Christian year.

For example, fasting on certain weekdays and on special holy days had long been a part of Jewish faith and life, and members of the first Christian communities continued the practice. In addition, Christians would join those preparing for baptism (called catechumens) in days of prayer and fasting during the weeks prior to their baptism at the Easter Vigil, and most intensively on the Friday and Saturday before Easter Sunday. Eventually these days of fasting, penitence, and preparation were combined and solidified into the Lenten season of forty days that we know today.

In a similar way, the calendar of saints' days evolved during the eras of persecution, in response to the growing need in the early church to commemorate the death of a Christian who died in witness to the faith. These martyrs were remembered both to honor their memory and to strengthen other Christians, who might be faced with persecution themselves. At first, these commemorations were probably for local witnesses to the faith, but as the church grew, the practice of remembering and celebrating the saints and martyrs became more widespread, especially during the

Middle Ages. The Reformation of the sixteenth century sought to remove some of the focus from the lives of the saints and place it instead on the celebration of the Sunday Eucharist. Anglicans still commemorate saints' days, though they never replace the Sunday celebration of Jesus' resurrection. Biographies of the saints commemorated in the Episcopal Church can be found in a book called *Lesser Feasts and Fasts,* which is updated every three years as new saints are added at our General Convention. It also provides Scripture readings and prayers that can be used to mark their feast days.

THE LECTIONARY

When the early Christians gathered for worship, prayer, and the reading of Scripture, they probably based their choice of readings on the Hebrew Scriptures used in the Jewish synagogues. Soon they began adding readings from Christian writings (such as the gospels and the letters of Paul and other apostles). Gradually, lectionaries—books containing the readings from the Bible selected for public worship—were developed to provide a pattern to these readings. As the church year took shape, readings with particular themes were assigned to certain feasts and holy days.[10]

The Old Testament, psalm, epistle, and gospel readings you hear during the Sunday Eucharist at an Episcopal church today are normally taken from the lectionary found at the back of The Book of Common Prayer. The current lectionaries for all the liturgical denominations today share common elements: ours is a revision of the lectionary adopted by the Roman Catholic Church after the Second Vatican Council in the 1960s.

The Episcopal lectionary is divided into a three-year cycle, called Years A, B, and C, based on the reading of the gospels. Most of the gospel readings come from Matthew in Year A, from Mark in Year B, and from Luke in Year C. The content of the Old Testament reading and the psalm is often linked to the gospel, while passages from the Epistles are usually simply read in order from week to week.

In addition to the Sunday readings, the prayer book lectionary also provides readings for saints' and holy days, and for various occasions. When you attend a special service such as a church convention or ordination, the readings from the Bible that you hear will be taken from this list.

TRADITIONS OF THE CHRISTIAN YEAR

Over the centuries many traditions have developed around the celebrations of the seasons, feasts, and fasts of the Christian calendar. Anglicans have received over two thousand years of these traditions, which have been compiled, practiced, and adapted for the formation of our faith, as well as for our enjoyment. As we participate in these traditions, we learn and experience what it means to be an Episcopalian.

One tradition that is widely practiced in the Episcopal Church today is to mark the change of seasons with the use of color. You may notice that as you move through the church year the color of the vestments worn by the clergy will differ according to the season. These vestments will include long fabric scarves called stoles, which are worn over white albs by the clergy (hanging straight down for the priests and bishops, from left to right for the deacons). In some congregations you will also see the colors change in the outer vestments, called the chasuble for the celebrant, the dalmatic for the deacon, and perhaps the tunicle for the subdeacon. The vestments will match or coordinate in color and design with the fabrics used to adorn the altar area: the altar frontal, which hangs in front of the altar, and the cloth hangings of matching fabric at the lectern and the pulpit.

The palette of colors we use today—including green, red, purple, white, and blue—is a relatively new tradition in the church. As recently as the eighteenth century, for example, colored vestments were rarely used in the Church of England. In the Eastern Orthodox churches brightly colored vestments have been used for centuries, but often with no particular connection to the season. During the Middle Ages parishes tended to use their finest vestments, regardless of the color, on feast days and their plainer ones on ordinary days. Some vestments at that time were even yellow and orange, colors now largely relegated to trimmings.[11]

It was not until the late nineteenth and early twentieth centuries that the current Roman Catholic system of associating certain colors with the seasons in the church year—purple with Lent, white with Easter and Christmas, purple or blue with Advent, green for the rest of the year—was adopted by the Episcopal Church. And since that time, as Anglicanism has become increasingly multicultural, the artistic traditions of other cultures and countries have enriched our palette of colors and designs. Today, you might see colorful stoles from Central America and brilliant altar frontals from Africa gracing the worship of American suburban churches.

One of the most significant recent events influencing today's church calendar has been the recovery of the liturgies and traditions of the early church, through the work of the liturgical movement in the twentieth century. The revisions to our 1979 Book of Common Prayer and *The Book of Occasional Services*,[12] for example, are the fruit of the efforts of a generation of scholars to recover the clarity, simplicity, and beauty of the early church's prayer and worship. The Easter Vigil, an ancient liturgy that is included for the first time in this prayer book, helps us understand that baptism was central to the theology and worship of the early church. The rites of the catechumenate, a time of formation for those preparing for baptism in the early church, are likewise restored in our *Book of Occasional Services,* adapted for modern use.

The recovery of the prayers and liturgies of the early church is important not because the worship of the early church was somehow "better" than that of later centuries, but because it was closer to the original source of that worship—the life, death, and resurrection of Jesus. The church's liturgies today are greatly enriched by this awareness of the traditions of the church in previous generations: many of us joined the Episcopal Church because of the beauty and depth of its worship, which seeks to combine the best traditions from every generation of the past two thousand years.

Like the repeating patterns created by my son Benjamin's Spirograph, in the repetition of these traditions year after year, our worship is united with the prayers of countless Christians throughout the ages, giving it a richness of texture, clarity, and meaning it could not have otherwise. We worship in time, offering our prayers and thanksgivings as the earth's seasons change from winter to spring to summer to fall. Yet, in the church's calendar, we also worship beyond time, aware that throughout the seasons of the church year we are repeating words and actions that Christians have repeated before us for generation upon generation, uniting us with them and the God who creates, loves, and redeems us all.

QUESTIONS FOR FURTHER THOUGHT AND DISCUSSION

1. How do you mark the passing of time and seasons in your family? What traditions do you keep year after year? Why? How did they develop and change over time?

2. What memories do you have of keeping the feasts and fasts of the church year as a child? If you were raised in another religious faith, what traditions did you keep every year? What traditions from your childhood would you like to pass on to your children and grandchildren?

3. Locate a copy of *Lesser Feasts and Fasts* and look through the calendar of saints. What names do you recognize? Are there names that surprise you? Find the saint for your birthday—or a saint you would like to know more about—and read his or her biography and collect.

4. Turn to the Lectionary in The Book of Common Prayer, beginning on page 888. Look through the propers listed for the Sundays in Years A, B, and C. What feast days do you recognize? Select a particular Sunday and compare the readings for each year. What themes do you see?

Advent

Merciful God, who sent your messengers the prophets to preach repentance and prepare the way for our salvation: Give us grace to heed their warnings and forsake our sins, that we may greet with joy the coming of Jesus Christ our Redeemer.

Collect for the Second Sunday of Advent (BCP 211)

When you walk into your parish church on the Sunday closest to November 30, you will probably notice some changes. The altar frontal will be either purple or blue, rather than the green of much of the summer and fall. The flowers at the altar may be more subdued or even absent. Somewhere in the church you may find a large evergreen wreath with four candles standing among the greenery, and before the service begins one of the candles will be lit. Something has changed: the season of Advent has begun.

ADVENT THEMES

The Christian calendar begins its new year not on January 1, but on the first Sunday of Advent—which is always four Sundays before Christmas (December 25) and the Sunday closest to St. Andrew's Day (November 30). Our word "Advent" derives

15

from the Latin *Adventus,* which means "coming," and originally referred just to the feast of Christmas. But over time the season of Advent took on a double meaning. Today it refers both to the "first coming" of Jesus Christ in his birth at Christmas, and to his "second coming" at the end of time.

For many of us today the weeks of December are filled—usually overfilled!—with activities and family traditions. Our days are packed with festive preparations: buying presents, baking cookies and breads, preparing for guests, decorating trees, and perhaps attending parties. So it can be disconcerting to find that when we arrive at church on the Sundays of Advent we encounter not only hopeful signs of the birth of the baby Jesus but also sober warnings about judgment at the end of time and a call to "forsake our sins" in preparation for Jesus' second coming. We celebrate the light of Christ coming into the world—but it comes to a world that is often broken and dark.

It is important to remember that Advent is not just a season in which we recall an event of the past—Jesus' birth—but also a time in which we look to the present and the future. When will Jesus come again? When will we see the kingdom of God on earth, as it is in heaven? Of course no one knows. And so the more important questions are: What can we do as the church, Christ's body here on earth, to bring about God's reign of justice and peace today? What can we do as individuals to reorder our lives, in the light of God's love? What would it mean to live as a people who believe in Jesus as the savior of all the earth and who expect him to come again at the fulfillment of time? Each Advent we turn to these questions anew.

It is easy to sentimentalize Advent and Christmas by focusing so much on the coming birth of the baby Jesus that we lose sight of why he came—to save a lost, sinful, and beloved people; to restore a broken world; to conquer death and raise all the creation to new life in God. We love anticipating happy events, and most of us would rather think about the birth of a baby than about restoring the world. Yet, the gospel loses its power and meaning when we gloss over the reality of darkness in our world.

I was enormously pregnant with my second child during Advent, and although I looked with joyful expectation to his coming birth in early January, at the same time I was keenly aware of the fragility of human life. Tragedies happen. Births go awry. An appalling number of children in our world do not survive infancy, and those who do often do not have clean water or enough to eat simply because those of us who have more than enough have not found a way to share with those who do not. We live in a broken world. And yet the gospel tells us that our brokenness cannot be separated from our redemption and renewal of life: even as we are forgiven, healed, restored, and raised to new life in the kingdom of God, we remain fragile, fallen human beings in this world. Advent holds all these aspects of our lives— hope and desolation, life and death, light and darkness, judgment and forgiveness, longing and fulfillment—together in one season.

ADVENT TRADITIONS

We first know of western Christians keeping the season of Advent in the sixth century, long after the Lent-Easter-Pentecost cycle had been established in the church calendar. Just as Lent was a time of preparation for Easter, Advent was kept as a season of fasting and preparation for Christmas. For this reason, at least since the later Middle Ages (when the use of liturgical colors became more widespread), purple has remained traditionally the solemn color of the altar hangings and vestments for Advent, just as in Lent. However, in recent years, many congregations have begun using blue, the color associated with Mary, because of her significance as the mother of Jesus. In most churches today Advent is kept more as a season of sober yet joyful anticipation than of penitence.

The Advent Wreath

The lighting of the Advent wreath is a beloved tradition in many congregations. The most likely origin of the lighted wreath is the Teutonic firewheel, which was a circle of evergreens with large candles or torches on top intended to honor the sun god.[13] The Christian Advent wreath is usually made of evergreen with four candles evenly spaced around the circle. The candles can be the color of the Advent vestments—purple or blue—or white. In some places, a rose or pink candle is used on the Third Sunday of Advent, following a Roman tradition of keeping that day as Gaudete (Latin for "rejoice") Sunday, because of the use of the antiphon "Rejoice in the Lord always" with the introit psalm.

Usually just before the service begins, an acolyte or other liturgical minister will light one candle for each Sunday of Advent, that is, one candle on the First Sunday of Advent, two on the Second Sunday, and so on. *The Book of Occasional Services* notes that "no special prayers or ceremonial elaboration . . . is desirable" (*BOS* 30), but in many congregations, prayers and responses at the lighting of the wreath are a cherished tradition. The Prayers for Light found in the prayer book (BCP 110–11) are particularly appropriate during evening services in Advent, and for family prayers around the Advent wreath at home.

The Advent wreath is "a visual symbol marking the progress of the season of Advent" (*BOS* 30), but it is also a powerful symbol of one of the themes of Advent: light that shines in the darkness. Especially in places where Advent is kept during the shortest days of winter, the warm glow of the Advent wreath is a welcome reminder of the light of the gospel.

Advent wreaths are also a good way to keep the season of Advent at home. Children in particular enjoy the rituals surrounding the lighting of candles and the "countdown to Christmas." In some congregations, people gather just before Advent begins for a festive time of wreath-making, using a variety of greens in smaller rings for table-top wreaths. For many years our family has used an Advent wreath-holder made of blue glazed ceramic pottery, and after being adorned with greens gathered from the trees and bushes in our yard, it becomes the centerpiece for our dinner table. Prayers at the lighting of the wreath are then incorporated into our grace before the evening meal each night throughout Advent and Christmas.

The Advent Calendar

Another way to mark the progress of Advent is the Advent calendar. These calendars come in a multitude of forms, from a simple paper calendar with flaps covering each of the days to fabric pockets on a background scene to painted wooden boxes with cubbies for small items. Again, many children enjoy this hands-on way of keeping Advent, and families can incorporate prayers and brief Scripture readings or nativity stories into the daily ritual of opening the Advent calendar. In our family we now have two calendars: one is made of fabric, with small cloth figures in numbered pockets that create a nativity scene when completed. The other is a wooden box with cubbies, and we place one piece of a wooden child's nativity scene in each cubby (as well as, I confess, a trinket or piece of candy or food). As Advent progresses our older son's crèche grows more detailed, and in the cubby for Christmas Day, we have the figure of the baby Jesus. His excitement in anticipating this ritual every morning is contagious and has become an important part of Advent in our family.

St. Nicholas

The feast day of Nicholas, a fourth-century bishop of Myra (a town on the Mediterranean in what is now known as Turkey), is remembered during Advent on December 6, offering families an opportunity to talk with their children about the origins of the Santa Claus tradition. Nicholas's biography in *Lesser Feasts and Fasts* notes that although we know very little about him, he may have been one of the bishops present at the Council of Nicaea in 325, which developed the Nicene Creed we affirm each Sunday. He suffered greatly during the persecution under the Roman emperor Diocletian, and in the Middle Ages was venerated as a patron saint of children in need. Dutch colonists in New York brought to this country the tradition of Nicholas—or Santa Claus, as he was popularly known—bearing gifts to children.

In our own day the story of Santa Claus has grown to mythical proportions, and many parents struggle with what to tell their children. In our family we celebrate the feast of St. Nicholas early in Advent by setting out small ceramic or cloth figurines of Bishop Nicholas we have collected over the years, giving small gifts to our children, and talking about his love of children. As children who believe in Santa Claus grow older and begin to question the story of a plump man in a red suit coming down their chimney with a sack of presents, they may find it helpful to know that there was in fact a real bishop who models for us a compassionate concern for children of all ages.

Advent Lessons and Carols

The English service of lessons and carols in Advent originated in Cornwall, in southern England, where Bishop Edward Benson created the liturgy to be sung at his cathedral in the city of Truro. In 1918, it was adapted by Eric Milner-White for use at Kings College, Cambridge, and in that form it has become a beloved tradition in many cathedrals and parishes in England and North America. In our *Book of Occasional Services* it is called an Advent Festival of Lessons and Music, and there you will find the beautiful Bidding Prayer, written by Milner-White, calling us to keep a holy Advent:

> Dear People of God: In the season of Advent, it is our responsibility and joy to prepare ourselves to hear once more the message of the Angels, to go to Bethlehem and see the Son of God lying in a manger. (*BOS* 32)

The prayer continues with intercessions for the needs of the world, for "the poor and helpless, the cold, the hungry and the oppressed, the sick and those who mourn, the lonely and unloved, the aged and little children" (*BOS* 33). Up to nine Scripture lessons follow the Bidding Prayer, interspersed with Advent hymns, carols, and canticles.

Usually a congregation will offer a service of Advent Lessons and Carols early in Advent as a wonderful way to enter into the season. Advent hymns, many of them familiar and beloved, are especially helpful in conveying the true meaning of this season.

"O Come, O Come, Emmanuel," for example, is a particularly well-known Latin hymn from the ninth century. Its verses capture with poetic richness the themes of Advent, making them worthy of consideration throughout these weeks:

> O come, O come, Emmanuel, and ransom captive Israel,
> that mourns in lonely exile here until the Son of God appear.
> Rejoice! Rejoice! Emmanuel shall come to thee, O Israel![14]

Another well-known Advent hymn filled with poetic images of light and darkness, waiting, and the fulfillment of redemption has echoes of the Advent readings from the prophet Isaiah and the gospels concerning John the Baptist:

> Comfort, comfort ye my people, speak ye peace, thus saith
>   our God;
> comfort those who sit in darkness mourning 'neath their
>   sorrows' load.
> Speak ye to Jerusalem of the peace that waits for them;
> tell her that her sins I cover, and her warfare now is over.
>
> Hark, the voice of one that crieth in the desert far and near,
> calling us to new repentance since the kingdom now is here.
> Oh, that warning cry obey! Now prepare for God away;
> let the valleys rise to meet him and the hills bow down to
>   greet him.[15]

The lessons provided in *The Book of Occasional Services* for this festival focus on the creation and re-creation (or redemption) of humankind, especially the words of the prophets proclaiming God's promises of a "new heaven and a new earth" through the coming of the Messiah.

THE SUNDAY LITURGY IN ADVENT

Probably the most obvious changes to the Sunday liturgy you will notice in Advent are the purple or blue vestments and altar hangings and the appearance of the Advent wreath. But as the service begins you will find other changes as well. You may be accustomed to singing one of arrangements for the *Gloria in excelsis* or another hymn of praise immediately after the opening prayer. In Advent, the *Kyrie eleison* ("Lord, have mercy") or the *Trisagion* ("Holy God, Holy and Mighty, Holy Immortal One, Have mercy upon us") is sung instead because of the more sober, penitential tone.

The Lectionary

The Scripture readings for the season of Advent focus on three biblical figures that play important roles in the preparation for Christ's coming: the prophet Isaiah, John the Baptist, and Mary the mother of Jesus.

The various prophecies of the coming King and Savior found in the book of the prophet Isaiah have long been interpreted by Christians as referring to Jesus. Perhaps the most well-known reading is the sign given to Ahaz that "the young woman is with child and shall bear a son, and shall name him Immanuel" (Isaiah 7:14). Matthew quotes this passage in his gospel, seeing Jesus' birth to the young girl Mary as the fulfillment of "what had been spoken by the Lord through the prophet" (Matthew 1:22).

Other passages from Isaiah are equally important to the message of Advent.

> *He shall not judge by what his eyes see,*
> *or decide by what his ears hear;*
> *but with righteousness he shall judge the poor,*
> *and decide with equity for the meek of the earth. . . .*

> *The wolf shall live with the lamb,*
> *the leopard shall lie down with the kid,*
> *the calf and the lion and the fatling together,*
> *and a little child shall lead them. . . .*

> *They will not hurt or destroy on all my holy mountain;*

for the earth will be full of the knowledge of the L*ORD*
as the waters cover the sea. (Isaiah 11:3–4, 6, 9)

This is the Advent hope, of a world where there is justice for
the poor and meek, where violence is no more, where former
enemies live together in peace, where even little children are safe
and secure.

Christians have also long associated Isaiah's prophecies with
the figure of John the Baptist:

> *In those days John the Baptist appeared in the wilderness of*
> *Judea, proclaiming, "Repent, for the kingdom of heaven has come*
> *near." This is the one of whom the prophet Isaiah spoke when he*
> *said,*
> *"The voice of one crying out in the wilderness:*
> *'Prepare the way of the Lord, make his paths straight.'"*
> (Matthew 3:1–3)

John the Baptist lived for years in the Palestinian desert, a land of
arid plains, rocky canyons, and steep cliffs, a place of great loneliness and danger from bandits and wild animals. It was in the
desert that John, "like the Old Testament prophets before him
and Christian hermits after him, would learn to live with the elements, with himself, and with God."[16] There is something about
the starkness of the desert that helps us understand things more
clearly, and when John returned to human society he was able to
speak with absolute certainty of the coming kingdom of God.
He saw the need for people to change their ways, to repent or
"turn around" to prepare the way for the One who was coming
soon.

We are so used to hearing about John the Baptist that we cannot imagine the story of Jesus' life without him. But what would
it have been like for Mary without John's mother, Elizabeth?
What would it have been like for Jesus without John? Would
people have listened to Jesus without John having prepared the
way?

> *As the people were filled with expectation, and all were question-*
> *ing in their hearts concerning John, whether he might be the*
> *Messiah, John answered all of them by saying, "I baptize you*
> *with water; but one who is more powerful than I is coming."*
> (Luke 3:15–16)

Luke's phrase "the people were filled with expectation" caught my attention one Advent several years ago, and every Advent I am reminded again of how important it is to live "filled with expectation." When we do not have hope we do not have a future, and even the present moment grows dim, closed in on itself. John the Baptist caused a stir with his strange diet, his odd wardrobe, and his acerbic words. He drew people out of their ordinary routines and made them question everything they accepted as normal—their religious practices and leaders; their social, ethical, and legal structures; their governing authorities. John was the messenger, urging them to expect something new, someone who would make crooked paths straight and rough ways smooth. And each Advent John urges us to do the same, to be a people "filled with expectation."

We encounter the third major figure in the Scripture lessons of Advent, Mary the mother of Jesus, on the fourth Sunday of Advent. On that Sunday we hear the gospel story of Mary's visit to her relative Elizabeth, still pregnant with John the Baptist. It is during that visit that she speaks the words that have become known as the *Magnificat* (the first word of the Latin translation): "My soul magnifies the Lord, and my spirit rejoices in God my Savior" (Luke 1:46–55). Anglicans know the *Magnificat* primarily from its frequent use in Morning and Evening Prayer: a multitude of beautiful settings to the *Magnificat* have been part of the Anglican musical tradition since the Reformation.

Mary's words help us understand who she thought her son was going to be, but they were also spoken out of her religious tradition: the *Magnificat* echoes the words another Hebrew woman, Hannah, prayed after she had given birth to her long-awaited first-born son, the prophet Samuel: "My heart exults in the LORD;

my strength is exalted in my God" (1 Samuel 2:1–10). Jesus was conceived, born, and raised within a religious tradition, and although he sometimes stood against practices within that tradition, he saw himself as the fulfillment of its prophetic hopes and yearnings for salvation. Mary raised him within that tradition, teaching him of the God who "has brought down the powerful from their thrones, and lifted up the lowly." As Jesus grew older she prayed with him to the God who "has helped his servant Israel, in remembrance of his mercy" and taught him of the "promise he made to our ancestors, to Abraham and his descendants forever." In Jesus' life and teaching we see echoes of Mary's *Magnificat,* with its resonance of the entire history of Jewish faith. For Christians, the church remains part of that faith tradition, the people of God seeking to follow the Savior whom we believe has come into the world and whose birth we will very soon celebrate on Christmas Day.

The Blessings

The Book of Occasional Services provides blessings that are appropriate for each of the seasons of the church year. At the conclusion of the Sunday Eucharists in Advent you may hear the priest or bishop bless the congregation with these or similar words, calling us once again to prepare the way for Christ's coming.

> May Almighty God, by whose providence our Savior Christ came among us in great humility, sanctify you with the light of his blessing and set you free from all sin. *Amen.*

> May he whose second Coming in power and great glory we await, make you steadfast in faith, joyful in hope, and constant in love. *Amen.*

> May you, who rejoice in the first Advent of our Redeemer, at his second Advent be rewarded with unending life. *Amen.* (*BOS* 22)

QUESTIONS FOR FURTHER THOUGHT AND DISCUSSION

1. Think about the times in your life when you have had to wait for something or for someone. How did it feel to wait? What was particularly difficult about waiting patiently? Did you find you could wait with hopeful expectation? What helped you pass the time?

2. What Advent traditions have you kept in your family? What traditions would you like to incorporate into your family life this year?

3. How has your understanding of Advent changed over the years?

4. Locate a copy of *The Book of Occasional Services* and turn to the Seasonal Blessings, beginning on page 22. Read the blessings for Advent. What Advent themes do you hear?

5. Think about the three biblical figures who are featured prominently in Advent—the prophet Isaiah, John the Baptist, and Mary the mother of Jesus. What do you know about them? What questions do you have about who they were and what they did?

3
Christmas

*Almighty God, you have given your only-begotten Son to take
our nature upon him, and to be born this day of a pure virgin:
Grant that we, who have been born again and made your
children by adoption and grace, may daily be renewed by your
Holy Spirit.*

Collect for the Nativity of Our Lord (BCP 213)

The challenge for most Christians today is not *whether* to
celebrate Christmas, but how to find its meaning as a feast of
the church. Christmas has become an increasingly popular winter festival in our secular society, and every year we are faced
with an array of opportunities to mark the event, from caroling
concerts and *Messiah* sing-alongs to offices parties and cut-your-
own Christmas trees. And as early as October we encounter the
trappings of Christmas every time we enter a shopping mall.

We can also participate in the simple, pleasurable activities
that connect us to our heritage, our family, and our friends.
Many of the traditions we associate with Christmas came to the
United States with our forbearers from other countries: decorating an evergreen tree with lights and garlands and bright tinsel
inside the house, going from door to door singing Christmas

carols to our neighbors, taking sleigh rides, exchanging gifts, hanging stockings by the fireplace. Some of these traditions have roots in the Christian faith; others are simply a way to share our nostalgia for days long gone, or our common hope of a just and peaceful society in which the dreams of children come true.

In our culture, we love Christmas, and we want to extend its celebration as long as possible. My five-year-old son will ask to watch a Christmas video even in summer. I recently noticed an advertisement for a concert in Washington, D.C., called "Christmas in August": the organizers of the event promised the concert of carols and favorite songs of the season would not be snowed out. Even the United States Postal Service recognizes the dual nature of Christmas celebrations today when it offers two designs for Christmas stamps, one religious (usually a medieval painting of Mary) and the other secular (usually a cheerful winter scene). Everyone seems to be "in" on the celebration—though it is not always clear *what* exactly we are celebrating. Perhaps we are celebrating many different things at one time.

Celebrating Christmas as a feast with multiple meanings is by no means a new phenomenon. Since Jesus' actual birthday was not something the earliest church held in remembrance, western Christians in the fourth century decided to adopt December 25 as their feast of Jesus' birth. This was the day that the Romans celebrated the birthday of the "unconquerable Sun," a festival in honor of the sun god Mithra, a deity of Persian origin. The festival was linked to the winter solstice and was a day marked by joyful celebration and great splendor in Rome, making it a fitting date for Christians to celebrate the birth of their own "unconquerable Son."[17] So from the very beginning Christmas has shared its day with celebrations from other religions. It remains for many people, from regular churchgoers to nonbelievers, a favorite festivity.

CHRISTMAS THEMES

For the church, Christmas is a time to celebrate the birth of Jesus in Bethlehem. We celebrate this birth not because Jesus was simply a "good man" but because we believe Jesus was—and is— both the human son of Mary and the divine Son of God. That makes Christmas a time to reflect on a mystery that the church calls the doctrine of the Incarnation. This important theological term comes from the Latin word *carne,* which means "flesh," and has to do with the divine taking on human flesh and coming among us in human form.

All religions throughout the ages have struggled with the fundamental question of the relationship between God and creation. Some believe in a God who is completely and utterly separate and distinct from humankind; others believe in a God who occasionally makes transitory, purely spiritual connections with certain individuals; still others believe in many gods who are present within all of creation, including human beings.

The early church struggled with this question, too. After centuries of heated debate the church formally defined the doctrine of the Incarnation at the Council of Chalcedon in 451. The church fathers tried to explain their conviction that Jesus was "at once complete in Godhead and complete in manhood, truly God and truly man" (BCP 864). What this meant was that Jesus was not just a man whom the Spirit of God visited on occasion (as with the Old Testament prophets), nor was he really God just pretending to be human. In either of these cases, the church fathers believed, it would not have been possible for Jesus to bring salvation to humankind. He must be *both* God *and* human to be our savior. In one of his Christmas sermons Augustine, the fifth-century bishop of Hippo, described it this way:

> Beloved, our Lord Jesus Christ, the eternal creator of all things, today became our Savior by being born of a mother. Of his own will he was born for us today, in time, so that he could lead us to his Father's eternity. God became human like us so

that we might become God. The Lord of the angels became one of us today so that we could eat the bread of angels.[18]

The Incarnation is absolutely central to the Christian faith. And yet at some level it must remain a mystery, and at Christmas it is often celebrated through the images and language of the poet rather than the theologian. The words to a Christmas hymn written only a few decades before the council at Chalcedon make much the same point, beautifully conveying the intersection of time and eternity, Godhead and humanity, in the birth and life of Jesus:

Of the Father's love begotten, ere the worlds began to be,
he is Alpha and Omega, he the source, the ending he,
of the things that are, that have been, and that future years
    shall see,
evermore and evermore!

O that birth for ever blessed, when the Virgin, full of grace,
by the Holy Ghost conceiving, bore the Savior of our race;
and the Babe, the world's Redeemer, first revealed his
    sacred face,
evermore and evermore![19]

In addition to the central theme of the "first coming" of Christ in the Incarnation, at Christmas you will hear echoes of another theme so prominent during Advent: the light of Christ coming into the darkness of our broken world. It is difficult for us today to imagine Christmas without candles. By now the Advent wreath is fully ablaze, and on Christmas Eve a fifth, white "Christmas candle" is often lighted in the middle of the wreath. Most congregations hold a midnight mass, filled with candlelight, on Christmas Eve. Even the collects for the Christmas season speak of the light of Christ:

O God, you have caused this holy night to shine with the brightness of the true Light: Grant that we, who have known the mystery

of that Light on earth, may also enjoy him perfectly in heaven.
(BCP 212)

Almighty God, you have poured upon us the new light of your
incarnate Word: Grant that this light, enkindled in our hearts,
may shine forth in our lives. (BCP 213)

Beloved and familiar hymns likewise convey the same theme of
Christ's light overcoming the darkness:

Silent night, holy night,
Son of God, love's pure light
radiant beams from thy holy face,
with the dawn of redeeming grace,
Jesus, Lord, at thy birth.
Jesus, Lord, at thy birth.[20]

CHRISTMAS SERVICES

Most congregations offer at least two services on Christmas
Eve: one in the afternoon or early evening, and one closer to midnight. This tradition of holding services on the eve of a feast is
derived from the Jewish practice of marking the start of a day the
evening before; likewise, in our Roman calendar a day begins at
midnight. Many congregations also offer a simple celebration on
Christmas Day.

Whichever service you choose to attend, your nose may tell
you something has changed even before you enter the church. As
you look around you will probably see garlands of greenery decorating the walls and area around the altar, their pungent evergreen scent filling the church. You may also see a bevy of winter
flowers, often red and rose-colored poinsettias, around the altar
and pulpit. The Advent wreath has been refreshed with new
greens and candles, and perhaps a white Christmas candle in the
center has joined the circle of light. Gone are the purple or
Sarum blue altar hangings and vestments, replaced by brilliant
white.

In many places the early service is a "family service" at which children may participate in a pageant telling the story of the nativity or sharing in the procession to the crèche. There are many different ways to do a Christmas pageant, from a simple retelling by the children of the story of Jesus' birth to an elaborate reenactment complete with stable scenery and live animals.

Another tradition in many parishes is the Christmas Eve procession to the crèche, often held during the early service. *The Book of Occasional Services* provides a form for prayers and simple responses said as the ministers of the service enter and pause at the Christmas crèche, which can be life-size or quite small (*BOS* 36–37). The origin of the practice of creating a manger scene at this season is attributed to St. Francis of Assisi, when in 1223 he built a crèche at Grecchia in Italy and it quickly became a widespread tradition in homes and churches. On Christmas Eve the figure of the baby Jesus may be carried in procession and placed in the crèche beside the figures for Mary and Joseph, along with the shepherds and animals that may be part of the scene. (The three wise men, however, should remain apart from the crèche until the feast of the Epiphany.)

The Lectionary

There are three sets of Scripture readings assigned for Christmas Day, and congregations are free to select which set seems appropriate in a given year. The Old Testament readings are from the book of the prophet Isaiah, and many of the passages are familiar (in an earlier translation) because they have been set to hymns and carols, as well as to music as glorious as Handel's *Messiah*:

> *For a child has been born for us,*
>   *a son given to us;*
> *authority rests upon his shoulders;*
>   *and he is named*
> *Wonderful Counselor, Mighty God,*
>   *Everlasting Father, Prince of Peace.* (Isaiah 9:6)

For the gospel reading, every year at Christmas we hear either the familiar story of Jesus' birth in Bethlehem as told by Luke or the passage from the beginning of John's gospel proclaiming the meaning of Jesus' birth—the Incarnation. The nativity story with which we are all familiar is actually a blending of two stories: one told in the gospel according to Luke, and the other in Matthew.

In that region there were shepherds living in the fields, keeping watch over their flock by night. Then an angel of the Lord stood before them, and the glory of the Lord shone around them, and they were terrified. But the angel said to them, "Do not be afraid; for see—I am bringing you good news of great joy for all the people: to you is born this day in the city of David a Savior, who is the Messiah, the Lord." (Luke 2:8–11)

Matthew continues the birth narrative with the story of the wise men coming from the East; that reading is usually included in church services on the feast of the Epiphany.

For many people the story of the nativity is a beloved account of the history of the birth of the Savior of the world and a foundational part of their faith. For others, the miraculous birth, with its virgin mother and angels and wise men and brilliant star, seems a fanciful legend that cannot be true in any historical, literal sense. The Reformation scholar Roland Bainton, in his introduction to a collection of Martin Luther's Christmas sermons, comments:

Luther rightly discerned that the greatest difficulty does not lie at the point of science, new or old. The deepest incredibility for him was not mechanical but moral. The question was not whether God could or would make a special star, but why the Lord of all the universe should care enough about us mortals to take our flesh and share our woes. The condescension of God was the great wonder.[21]

We cannot know exactly what happened in a historical sense at Jesus' birth, but at least for Martin Luther, as for many of us today, that knowledge is not the most important part of the Christmas message. Perhaps there were indeed shepherds and stars and angels; perhaps the story happened exactly as the gospel writers recorded it. Or perhaps the stories that developed in the very early church around the birth of Jesus were simply one of the ways those first Christians proclaimed their conviction that Jesus was a person of overwhelming significance: the long-awaited Messiah, who would bring a new creation in which the lion would lie down with the lamb. In either case, the wonderful truth is that God loved us enough to become one of us, to be born and live and die among us.

So it is important that in addition to the nativity story from Luke we also hear the reading from John's gospel. In this passage we hear the *meaning* of Christmas, apart from its historical narrative:

> *In the beginning was the Word, and the Word was with God, and the Word was God. . . . And the Word became flesh and lived among us, and we have seen his glory, the glory as of a father's only son, full of grace and truth.* (John 1:1, 14)

In John's prologue we hear the mystery of the Incarnation, the wonder of the God who created the world coming to live among us in human flesh, to take our nature upon him in order to restore a broken world and raise us up to new life.

In some congregations, the narrative from Luke is the gospel reading just prior to the sermon, and the passage from John is read at the end of the service from the back of the church, as the people kneel in candlelight following the singing of "Silent Night" or another favorite Christmas carol.

THE TWELVE DAYS OF CHRISTMAS

Most of us are familiar with the traditional Christmas carol detailing the elaborate and fanciful gifts received on the twelve days of Christmas. Yet the twelve days of Christmas are quite real: they are the days between the Feast of the Nativity on December 25 and the Feast of the Epiphany on January 6. On these days, in addition to the first and sometimes the second Sunday after Christmas (if there is one that year), the church marks a number of holy days.

Immediately after Christmas Day the church celebrates the feasts of two saints. On December 26 we remember St. Stephen, who was one of the seven people chosen by the apostles to tend to the church's care for widows and the poor. He thus was among the first to do what later became associated with the work of deacons in the church. His powerful preaching of the gospel led to his death by stoning at the hands of the Sanhedrin, the Jewish "supreme court" of Jesus' day. Although Stephen's feast day probably was kept in Jerusalem even before the celebration of Christmas, Christians moved his commemoration to December 26 since they thought it more suitable to remember the church's first martyr on the first day after the feast of the Nativity.

The following day, December 27, we celebrate the feast of St. John, the apostle and evangelist who was one of the inner circle of Jesus' disciples. He or his community wrote the gospel from which we read on Christmas Eve, as well as several letters and the Revelation to John.

Then on December 28 we remember the Holy Innocents, those male children in Bethlehem under the age of two who were killed by the soldiers of King Herod in his search for the baby Jesus. This feast is a harsh and jarring reminder of the cruel and violent world into which Jesus was born and in which we still live. It is a day for contemplating the reasons we are in need of a savior.

The Holy Name

In earlier prayer books January 1, marking the day on which Jesus was named, was called the Feast of the Circumcision. It was celebrated on this day because Luke's gospel tells us that Jesus was circumcised on the eighth day after his birth, according to Jewish custom (Luke 2:21). By either name, this feast has a long history in Christian tradition: it originated in the sixth century as a day for fasting, in opposition to pagan festivities celebrating the new year. Today this feast is still largely eclipsed for most of us by our own festivities marking the change of the yearly calendar, from New Year's Eve parties to football games on New Year's Day. But on this first day of the new year it can be a fruitful exercise to meditate on the practice of naming and to reflect on the ways our name connects us to our identity as it unfolds and develops over the years.

In the biblical world, a person's name revealed his or her character and essential nature. Jesus' name, the Greek version of the Hebrew name Joshua, means "the Lord saves." So when Jews in Jesus' day heard his name, they would know something about his mission to be an instrument of God's saving action in the world.[22] It has always been a source of some amusement in my family that I was named after a horse my mother loved when she was a child. But with each new year I have come to appreciate more the affection my mother had for her horse Vicki, and to see in her act of naming me a desire to express the loving connection a mother can have with her children. On the feast of the Holy Name I glimpse how my mother's love in naming me is merely an echo of the love of a God who also knew me before I was born.

Christmas Lessons and Carols

Some congregations offer the service in *The Book of Occasional Services* for a Christmas Festival of Lessons and Music on the first or second Sunday after Christmas, or on another evening during the twelve days of Christmas. Like the Advent service of lessons and carols, this festival begins with a Bidding Prayer:

> Dear People of God: In this Christmas Season, let it be our duty and delight to hear once more the message of the Angels, to go to Bethlehem and see the Son of God lying in a manger. (*BOS* 39)

Up to nine lessons then follow, interspersed with Christmas anthems, carols, and hymns. These Scripture readings focus more on the New Testament witness concerning the fulfillment of the words of the prophets in the birth and life of Jesus.

Offering a service of lessons and carols during the twelve days of Christmas provides an opportunity for us to hear the Christmas message again in the cold light of day, after the candles have been extinguished, the Christmas turkey has been turned into leftovers, the presents have been opened, and the guests have gone home. We sing beloved hymns and carols once more, with the flurry of activity over and the pressure of expectations lessened as we enter a new year. And we marvel again at their message of salvation.

In the relative quiet of the week or two following Christmas, we will pick up our ordinary lives again. During these twelve days of Christmas we can rest and reflect more deeply on the message proclaimed by the angel who brought "good news of great joy for all the people." No doubt most of us will have sung the popular Christmas carol "O Little Town of Bethlehem" at some point during the Christmas celebrations. The last two verses may hold an important clue as to how our wistful hope for a world in which there is "Christmas in August" and where there is "good will toward all" might in fact become a reality.

Where children pure and happy pray to the blessed Child,
where misery cries out to thee, Son of the mother mild;
where charity stands watching and faith holds wide the door,
the dark night wakes, the glory breaks, and Christmas comes
    once more.

O holy Child of Bethlehem, descend to us, we pray;
cast out our sin and enter in, be born in us today.
We hear the Christmas angels the great glad tidings tell;
O come to us, abide with us, our Lord Emmanuel![23]

Questions for Further Thought and Discussion

1. What memories do you have of Christmas as a child? What traditions are most meaningful in your family now? How do they relate to Christmas as a Christian feast day?

2. How do you feel about the early church's practice of "adopting" the celebrations of other religious traditions and making them Christian feast days? Can you think of ways the church continues to give Christian meanings to secular or national holidays today?

3. Have you ever kept the Twelve Days of Christmas? If so, how? What traditions could you incorporate into your family life this year that would help you celebrate the entire Christmas season?

4. Locate a copy of *The Hymnal 1982* and look at the section for Christmas (hymns 77–115). Choose one or two of your favorite Christmas hymns and describe why you find them particularly meaningful.

5. The feast of the Holy Name is one of the Twelve Days of Christmas. Do you know how and why your parents chose your name? Do you think your name fits you? What does your name tell others about you?

The Epiphany

O God, by the leading of a star you manifested your only Son to the peoples of the earth: Lead us, who know you now by faith, to your presence, where we may see your glory face to face.

Collect for the Feast of the Epiphany (BCP 214)

The feast of the Epiphany is celebrated in the western church on January 6, marking the end of the twelve days of the Christmas season. Epiphany is the third and final feast day of the Advent-Christmas-Epiphany cycle of the church year. If you are wondering what this feast is about, you have good reason: it usually falls on a weekday so we can miss its celebration if we attend church only on Sundays. And to further complicate matters, the meaning of the feast of the Epiphany has changed and evolved over the centuries, with different churches focusing on different themes.

You may thus be surprised to learn that Epiphany is probably an older feast than Christmas: it originated in the second or third century in the eastern church,[24] where it is still a celebration of the manifestation of Jesus as the Messiah at his baptism in the river Jordan by John the Baptist. For centuries it was one of the three major feasts of the church (along with Easter and Pentecost). Clearly, it has lost its primacy in our culture—very few businesses are closed on January 6 to mark the Epiphany, as they are on Christmas—and even many regular churchgoers are uncertain of its significance. However, since the revision of the prayer book in 1979 the themes of the Epiphany and the weeks that follow have been incorporated more and more into the life of the congregation. Now we think of Epiphany as a conclusion to the celebration of Christmas, a time for thoughtfully putting away the trimmings and trappings of Christmas by moving on to incorporate its message in our daily lives.

EPIPHANY THEMES

Epiphany is a Greek word meaning "manifestation, showing forth, revelation." This feast proclaims our faith that in Jesus, God is revealed to all people—not just to an inner circle or a chosen few, but to all people, in all places, and throughout all time. Christians believe that in the person of Jesus we see who God is, and in the words and actions of Jesus we see God at work in the world. The Epiphany marks a series of occasions at which Jesus was revealed to be God's Son.

The Epiphany and the weeks following that feast are a time in which we reflect on several "manifestations" of Jesus, as he was recognized as the Messiah (or Christ) by many different people. We hear about Jesus' baptism in the river Jordan by John the Baptist and the visit of the magi, or wise men, who followed the star to Bethlehem at Jesus' birth. We share the amazement of the guests at the wedding party at Cana, as Jesus performs his first miracle by turning water into fine wine. And we see Jesus' glory shown to three of his disciples on the mountain, as he is transfigured before them in a blaze of light. At the time of the English Reformation in the sixteenth century, as Archbishop Thomas Cranmer and the reformers arranged the prayer book, he assigned three readings for January 6: the baptism of Jesus at Morning Prayer, the visit of the magi at the Eucharist, and the wedding feast at Evensong. Since today it is rare to find a parish in which Episcopalians attend three services in one day, we now hear these readings on the Sundays following Epiphany.

Just as in Advent and Christmas, one of the primary themes of Epiphany is light. "Advent begins in darkness and moves toward light with the lighting of the Advent candles," the noted educator Joseph Russell explains. "Christmas proclaims the presence of the light. Epiphany calls us to spread the light."[25] Epiphany is also known as the Feast of Lights, as we continue our Christmas celebration of Christ as the light of the world:

> *What has come into being in him was life, and the life was the light of all people. The light shines in the darkness, and the darkness did not overcome it.* (John 1:3–5)

Likewise, in the Old Testament reading for the Epiphany we hear the Jewish hope for the restoration of Jerusalem described in images of light:

> *Arise, shine; for your light has come,*
> *   and the glory of the LORD has risen upon you. . . .*
> *Nations shall come to your light,*
> *   and kings to the brightness of your dawn. . . .*
> *They shall bring gold and frankincense,*
> *   and shall proclaim the praise of the LORD.* (Isaiah 60:1, 3, 6)

THE FEAST OF THE EPIPHANY

"In the time of King Herod, after Jesus was born in Bethlehem of Judea," the evangelist Matthew writes, "wise men from the East came to Jerusalem, asking, 'Where is the child who has been born king of the Jews? For we observed his star at its rising, and have come to pay him homage'" (Matthew 2:1–2). The story of the wise men is at the heart of the feast of the Epiphany, as it concludes the Christmas story of Jesus' birth.

In the Middle Ages the magi were associated with three kings and even given names—Melchior, Caspar, and Balthazar. Magi were astrologers, educated people who "studied the movement of the stars to interpret their meaning."[26] Matthew describes the gifts they brought to the newborn infant Jesus as gold (for royalty, emphasizing the kingship of Christ), frankincense (a tree gum burned during worship to produce an aromatic smoke, symbolizing prayer), and myrrh (a bitter resin used to anoint bodies before burial, foretelling Christ's death). In some congregations you will see a procession of the magi during the service, either some sort of pageant involving children or adults in costume, or the carrying of the figures of the magi to the Christmas crèche, which is then taken down after this service.

Another primary theme of the Epiphany, the celebration of Christ as the light of the world, permeates our Epiphany hymns:

The people who in darkness walked have seen a glorious light; on them broke forth the heavenly dawn who dwelt in death and night.

To hail thy rising, Sun of life, the gathering nations come, joyous as when the reapers bear their harvest treasures home.[27]

The vestments and altar linens remain white, the festival color of light, just as for Christmas. After the Epiphany we remove the Christmas crèche, greenery, and Christmas trees from our churches and homes.

Like Christmas, the feast of the Epiphany is kept on a fixed date, which poses a problem for churches during those years when it does not fall on a Sunday. Although the prayer book insists Epiphany must be celebrated on January 6, it does allow the gospel passage concerning the visit of the magi to be read on the Second Sunday after Christmas, which gives those who are unable to attend a weekday service the opportunity to hear the conclusion to the nativity story. Some congregations offer an evening service on Epiphany, complete with candles and the procession of the wise men to the crèche.

Also like Christmas, the date for the feast of the Epiphany was deliberately chosen by the early church as a way of proclaiming faith in Jesus as the Son of the one true God, while living in the midst of a pluralistic culture that honored many gods, including the sun. The liturgical scholar Marion Hatchett explains:

> In Egypt, January 6 was celebrated as the winter solstice when the sun god made his appearance (epiphany) and was honored with light, water, and wine. The Christians chose this time as the feast of the incarnation and connected it with three Gospel stories: the coming of the Magi, the baptism of Jesus, and the wedding at Cana. Of these the baptism was the primary event.[28]

Thus very early in the church, the feast of the Epiphany became associated with Christian images of light, water, and wine, and especially baptisms. Today we celebrate the single feast of the Epiphany over a period of several weeks, beginning with the coming of the magi on January 6, followed by a feast celebrating the baptism of Christ.

THE BAPTISM OF OUR LORD

We celebrate Jesus' baptism on the first Sunday after the Epiphany. It was at Jesus' baptism that his identity as the beloved Son of God was first revealed to those who were following John the Baptist, and who would now become disciples of Jesus of Nazareth.

> *And when Jesus had been baptized, just as he came up from the water, suddenly the heavens were opened to him and he saw the Spirit of God descending like a dove and alighting on him. And a voice from heaven said, "This is my Son, the Beloved, with whom I am well pleased." (Matthew 3:16–17)*

This Sunday is one of four days in the calendar that the prayer book holds as "especially appropriate" for baptisms, along with the Easter Vigil, Pentecost, and All Saints' Day (see BCP 312). Many congregations celebrate this feast day by a festival in which they baptize new members and reaffirm the baptismal covenant.

One of the great gifts of the liturgical movement of the twentieth century is the recovery of baptism as the central and *corporate* sacrament of initiation into the Christian life. It is in our baptism that we are christened—made Christians. In the early church the preparation for baptism was similar to the preparation for ordination today: two or three years of intensive study, prayer, and formation (called the catechumenate) within the church community, culminating in a Holy Week retreat prior to an elaborate baptismal ritual at the Easter Vigil. Over time the years of preparation were shortened to weeks and then days, and the age of baptismal candidates decreased until nearly all were infants. Baptisms were relegated to private ceremonies in the afternoon or evening, with only the parents and godparents present. With the recovery of baptism in the 1979 Book of Common Prayer as the primary sacrament of new life in Christ, baptisms have been restored to their rightful place, celebrated by the entire community at the main Sunday morning Eucharist.

This Sunday is a good day for remembering our own baptisms, and renewing our baptismal vows. Most congregations give the newly baptized a candle during the service, and many families light these candles at home on this feast day, as well as on the anniversary of each person's baptism. Since many of us were baptized as infants and thus have no memory of the event, it is helpful to reflect on the meaning of the sacrament for us in our lives as adults through participating in the baptisms of others. How do we hear God's words to Jesus at the river Jordan spoken to us as well? In what ways do we know that we, too, are God's beloved children, with whom he is well pleased?

This is the last Sunday for white vestments. On this day the vestments remind us particularly of the white robes worn by the newly baptized in the early church, and in some places still worn by baptismal candidates today. As they rose from the waters of baptism they were dried and anointed with aromatic oils, and dressed in the white robes signifying their redemption and new life.

THE SUNDAYS AFTER THE EPIPHANY

During the weeks after the festive celebrations of Christmas, the Epiphany, and the baptism of Christ we enter a time in late January and February when we hear the gospel stories of Jesus' first miracle at Cana and the beginning of his ministry in Galilee, and conclude with the story of the transfiguration. The number of Sundays after the Epiphany varies from four to nine, according to the date of Easter (and therefore the date on which Lent must begin) each year. On the Last Sunday after the Epiphany we always recall another "manifestation" of Jesus' glory, the transfiguration.

When you come to church on the Second Sunday after the Epiphany you will immediately notice that the white vestments and altar linens are gone, probably replaced by green—or whatever color your parish uses for its "ordinary time." Green has been called the color of "the ongoing life of the church"[29] and most congregations use some shade of green during these weeks and during the weeks of summer and early fall, in the Season after Pentecost.

The Scripture lessons for these weeks focus on the early events in Jesus' ministry following his baptism, when his unique identity and calling began to be "manifest" to others. We hear of Jesus changing water into wine at the wedding feast in Cana, the "first of his signs" that "revealed his glory" (John 2:11). We visit the synagogue in Nazareth, where he identified himself with the anointed one of whom Isaiah spoke: "The Spirit of the Lord is upon me, because he has anointed me to bring good news to the poor" (Luke 4:18). We go to the Sea of Galilee to hear Jesus calling the crowds to "repent, for the kingdom of heaven has come near" (Matthew 4:17), and watch his disciples leave their fishing nets to follow him. And we sit among the multitudes of men, women, and children who gather around Jesus as we listen to his Sermon on the Mount, beginning with the Beatitudes: "Blessed are the poor in spirit, for theirs is the kingdom of heaven" (Matthew 5:3).

Finally, on the Last Sunday after the Epiphany, we go up a high mountain with Jesus, Peter, James, and John. There Jesus "was transfigured before them, and his face shone like the sun, and his clothes became dazzling white. . . . And from the cloud a voice said, 'This is my Son, the Beloved; with him I am well pleased; listen to him!'" (Matthew 17:2, 5). Thus on this last Sunday after the Epiphany we come full circle, and hear again the words of revelation and "epiphany" we heard at Jesus' baptism: "This is my Son, the Beloved."

HOLY DAYS IN EPIPHANY

There are a number of holy days that fall during the weeks after the Epiphany, and that have to do with the Epiphany themes of mission and manifestation. Three of them are "red letter days": the feasts of the Confession of St. Peter the Apostle (January 18), the Conversion of St. Paul the Apostle (January 25), and the Presentation of Our Lord Jesus Christ in the Temple (February 2).

The first two are now linked in many churches in a week of prayer for Christian unity, during which special services of prayer are offered for the mission of churches throughout the world. The confession of Peter and conversion of Paul are especially appropriate during the weeks after the Epiphany, as we reflect on our own call to make Jesus known to others. Shortly before the transfiguration, Jesus met with his disciples and asked them who they think he is. Peter was the first to confess his belief that Jesus is "the Messiah [or the Christ], the Son of the living God" (Matthew 16:15–16). The collect for this day on which we recall Peter's confession asks God to "keep your Church steadfast upon the rock of this faith, so that in unity and peace we may proclaim the one truth and follow the one Lord, our Savior Jesus Christ" (BCP 238). Paul likewise came to believe that Jesus was the Messiah, after he had a vision of Jesus as "a light from heaven, brighter than the sun" and heard his call to preach the gospel to the Gentiles: "I am sending you to open their eyes so that they may turn from darkness to light" (Acts 26:13, 17–18). In the collect for the feast marking the conversion of Paul we give thanks for "the preaching of your apostle Paul," which has "caused the light of the Gospel to shine throughout the world"

(BCP 238)—again highlighting the Epiphany theme of light shining in the darkness.

The third major feast in these weeks, the Presentation of Our Lord Jesus Christ in the Temple, is also called Candlemas because of the tradition of carrying candles in procession at the celebration of this feast. It was on this day that Jesus was presented in the temple in Jerusalem, according to the Jewish requirement for purification following childbirth set forth in the law of Moses. Mary and Joseph took Jesus to Jerusalem and presented him to the Lord, offering the sacrifice required in the law of "a pair of turtledoves or two young pigeons" (Luke 2:22–24). While they were in the temple they encountered Simeon and Anna, two prophets who saw in Jesus the long-awaited Messiah. Simeon had been told by the Holy Spirit he would see the Messiah before he died. When Simeon saw Jesus, he took Jesus in his arms and spoke the words that have become the church's canticle The Song of Simeon, included in the prayer book for Morning and Evening Prayer:

> *Master, now you are dismissing your servant in peace,*
>   *according to your word;*
> *for my eyes have seen your salvation,*
>   *which you have prepared in the presence of all peoples,*
> *a light for revelation to the Gentiles*
>   *and for glory to your people Israel.* (Luke 2:29–32)

Anna likewise recognized Jesus as the Messiah, and began "to speak about the child to all who were looking for the redemption of Jerusalem" (Luke 2:38). Thus Simeon and Anna stand alongside the shepherds and magi in proclaiming their belief that in the infant Jesus lying in the manger or resting in their arms, God was overcoming the darkness of this world with the glorious light of salvation.

EPIPHANY BLESSINGS

The blessings provided in *The Book of Occasional Services* for the Sundays after the Epiphany echo the events and themes of manifestation, light, and glory we have seen in the Scriptures and prayers of these weeks. They also make it clear that in Epiphany we not only look back to the ways in which Jesus' identity was made apparent to the people who knew him long ago, but we also look for Jesus in the liturgy and in our lives today.

> May Almighty God, who led the Wise Men by the shining of a star to find the Christ, the Light from Light, lead you also, in your pilgrimage, to find the Lord. *Amen.*

> May God, who sent the Holy Spirit to rest upon the Only-begotten at his baptism in the Jordan River, pour out that Spirit on you who have come to the waters of new birth. *Amen.*

> May God, by the power that turned water into wine at the wedding feast at Cana, transform your lives and make glad your hearts. *Amen.* (*BOS* 24)

QUESTIONS FOR FURTHER THOUGHT AND DISCUSSION

1. What Epiphany traditions do you keep every year (if any)? What traditions would you like to introduce into your family life now?

2. Jesus' baptism was a pivotal moment in his life and a "manifestation" of his identity as God's Son. If you are preparing for baptism now, how do you anticipate your baptism will affect your identity? If you were baptized as a child or adult, what do you remember about your own baptism? If you were baptized as an infant, have you heard stories about the event from your parents or godparents? How has your baptism affected who you are?

3. Think about times in your life when you have come to "see" differently, as if some previously hidden truth has been revealed to you. What led to that moment of transfiguration or manifestation? How did your life change because of it?

4. What do you think it means when Christians proclaim Jesus Christ to be the "light of the world"?

5. Read and reflect on the Epiphany blessings quoted in this chapter or found in *The Book of Occasional Services,* page 24. What Epiphany themes do you hear?

Lent

O God, whose glory it is always to have mercy: Be gracious to all who have gone astray from your ways, and bring them again with penitent hearts and steadfast faith to embrace and hold fast the unchangeable truth of your Word, Jesus Christ your Son.

Collect for the Second Sunday in Lent (BCP 218)

The word "Lent" conjures up a variety of images and feelings, often from childhood memories of being required to "keep a holy Lent." This generally meant no feasting, no parties, no fun; for some it also meant going to confession and fasting on certain days of the week. These weeks before Easter are popularly known as a season of sober self-denial, with an emphasis on repenting from sin and receiving God's forgiveness. In the cold climates of the northern United States and Canada, during the months of February and March it still grows dark in the afternoon. With cold, gray skies and snow or sleety rain falling sometimes even into April, this seems the perfect environment for keeping the rigors of a "holy Lent."

Figuring out how to keep a holy Lent can be a challenge, but if we move beyond the popular conceptions (and misconceptions), Lent holds the possibility for real change—or to use the church's word, conversion—in our lives, as well as for rich and lasting spiritual growth. The word "lent" comes from the Anglo-Saxon word *lencton,* referring to the springtime of the year when the days grow longer and warmer and brighter. It is during the weeks of Lent that (at least spiritually) we begin to emerge from our protective winter burrows, to stretch our legs and sniff the air for signs of new life.

Several years ago I heard the bishop of Massachusetts, M. Thomas Shaw, speak at the cathedral in Boston of his experience of being in the Holy Land for Lent that year. There it is summertime during the weeks before Easter, with the desert in full bloom, the trees laden with olives and figs, the hazy smell of ripe fruit and the sound of buzzing insects filling the air. As he moved through the days of prayer and reflection before Easter in the midst of such abundance and beauty he came to understand Lent as a time of being refreshed by a loving God instead of a time of arduous effort to improve. One of the prefaces for Lent—the part of the Eucharistic Prayer that varies according to the season— echoes this perspective of Lent as a time of refreshment, joy, and renewal:

> *You bid your faithful people cleanse their hearts, and prepare with joy for the Paschal feast; that, fervent in prayer and in works of mercy, and renewed by your Word and Sacraments, they may come to the fullness of grace which you have prepared for those who love you.* (BCP 379)

This is not to say that Lent is a season of giddy celebration, but rather that joy in the new life we have found in the Christian faith should never be overwhelmed by our struggles to live out that faith or our awareness of the ways we fall short. The ultimate purpose of Lent is to strengthen our spiritual lives. In Lent we step back and consider the ways we need to repent, to turn around—to be converted. I usually experience repentance as sorrow and grief followed by tremendous relief and a sense of "rightness," peace, and deep joy. It can feel like a dislocated knee or shoulder moving back into place. Repentance is not always pain-free, but it is the start of profound healing.

A friend of mine thinks of Lent as an annual spiritual check-up. He visits his doctor once a year to check on the state of his body: he rejoices in the ways it is healthy and he learns what steps he needs to take to repair those parts that need some medical attention or a little exercise. In the same way, during Lent we as individual Christians and as a church—the Body of Christ—consider our spiritual health. How are we living the gospel in our lives, our homes, our churches, our towns, our schools, our places of work? What areas of growth or signs of renewal should we celebrate with gratitude and joy? In what ways have we fallen short, grown stagnant or cold-hearted, or failed to love God by embracing new life when we encounter it? These are the kinds of questions we ask of ourselves during the weeks of Lent.

LENTEN THEMES

In the early church Lent began as a period of intense preparation for the baptisms that would be celebrated at the Easter Vigil, and eventually settled into a period of forty days (not counting Sundays, which are not considered part of the Lenten fast). The liturgy for Ash Wednesday explains it well in its invitation to "the observance of a holy Lent":

> *The first Christians observed with great devotion the days of our Lord's passion and resurrection, and it became the custom of the Church to prepare for them by a season of penitence and fasting. This season of Lent provided a time in which converts to the faith were prepared for Holy Baptism. It was also a time when those who, because of notorious sins, had been separated from the body of the faithful were reconciled by penitence and forgiveness, and restored to the fellowship of the Church.* (BCP 264–265)

This time of preparation for baptism became known as the catechumenate, from the Greek word for catechism, meaning to hear and instruct. In many places this was a lengthy opportunity for hearing the teaching of the bishop, studying the Scriptures, praying with the community of the faithful, fasting, and turning away from any profession, relationships, or activities that were not compatible with the Christian faith as the church understood it at that time.

The pilgrim Egeria, who traveled to Jerusalem from her convent in the west of Spain late in the fourth century and recorded her experiences of the Lent and Easter liturgies in a diary for her sister nuns, describes in some detail how the catechumenate worked in the Holy Land. She wrote that on the day before Lent began, those who wished to be baptized at Easter gave their names to the priest, who recorded them and read them to the bishop on the following day. The candidates appeared with their godmother or godfather, as well as neighbors who knew them. The bishop asked the witnesses about the candidate's way of life, inquiring, "Does this person lead a good life?" If anyone accused the candidate of something, the bishop ordered the person to go out: "Let such a one amend their life, and when this is done, then approach the baptismal font."[30]

The catechumens then received instruction in the faith for three hours a day for the next seven weeks, including study of the Bible, the doctrines of the church, and the creed. Catechumens joined the rest of the congregation for the first part of the service, and then were dismissed prior to the celebration of the Eucharist.

Today many congregations have sought to restore a similar period of formation for those who wish to be baptized, as well as for those baptized as infants who wish to renew their baptismal vows. If your congregation offers some form of the catechumenate, you may notice a variety of ways in which the preparation of and prayer for catechumens is included in your Sunday liturgies during Lent. In any case, you will probably notice more opportunities for Bible study, teaching about the Christian faith, and shared prayer during these weeks.

The catechumenate is important not only for those who are to be baptized. It also helps the congregation to recover the primary focus of Lent: the meaning of our baptism. It is interesting to note that the only reason Lent was connected with Easter in the early church was that the Easter Vigil was the primary occasion for baptisms. It was not until much later that Lent came to be associated with Jesus' forty-day fast in the wilderness and his suffering and death at Passover.

The service for Ash Wednesday, the first day of Lent, introduces several related themes of Lent, including penitence (or sorrow) for our sins, repentance and conversion, human mortality, and eternal life. But Lent is not a long, dark, somber Ash Wednesday. While Lent gives us the chance to confess and turn away from sinful patterns or actions and encourages us to reflect on the reality of human suffering and death, it is much more than that. If the primary focus of Lent is preparation for a renewal of our baptismal vows at Easter and reconciliation through the forgiveness of sin, then Lenten themes also include other aspects of the Christian life that help us to grow in faith, such as prayer, Bible study, and caring for those in need.

LENTEN TRADITIONS

One tradition many of us grew up with is the custom of "giving up" something for Lent—like chocolate or alcohol or sweets. This modified fast is rooted in the very early Jewish and Christian practice of fasting on certain days of the week and on holy days throughout the year. In some places, especially in the desert and medieval monastic communities, Lent was indeed kept as a forty-day fast, though acceptance of the practice in parishes seems not to have been widespread even then. In the Middle Ages the keeping of a Lenten fast became associated with Jesus' forty-day fast in the desert following his baptism. Today the church encourages us to fast on Ash Wednesday and Good Friday during Lent, and many find this way of expressing their Lenten devotion through their bodies very helpful for cleansing the mind and focusing the soul.

Another approach to keeping Lent is to "take on" a spiritual discipline or practice. Some find it is not what they eat or drink that is separating them from God, but their lack of time spent in prayer or study, their neglect of worship, their self-centeredness in relationships, or the ways they spend their time or money or energy. For them, making a commitment to spend a half-hour a day in prayer, or to attend a Bible study once a week, or to devote an evening or weekend to doing something special for a friend or spouse, or to take a meal to a homeless shelter can be a useful Lenten discipline. Lent can thus be a time for clearing away those things that stand in the way to a vibrant spiritual life, as well as a time for adding practices in prayer, study, and outreach that lead to God.

Spiritual Disciplines

Because Lent is integrally connected to the meaning of our baptism and our formation in the Christian faith, today our parishes tend to have an abundance of classes, adult forums, prayer groups, book groups, Bible studies, retreats and quiet days, and opportunities for fasting, confession, and spiritual direction. These and many other ways of growing in the Christian faith are sometimes called "spiritual disciplines." They have developed in the church over the centuries in a number of cultures and across various religious traditions. Christian ways of prayer, for example, emerged from Jewish traditions but were quickly shaped by the Greek, Roman, Egyptian, North African, Anglo-Saxon, and Celtic cultures in which Christianity grew. In our multicultural world today we are the recipients of a wealth of spiritual disciplines from Buddhism, Taoism, Islam, and Hinduism as well.

During Lent you may be exposed to a number of spiritual disciplines and opportunities for growth, some of which will "fit" your spiritual journey and some of which will not. Some may help sustain your growth in faith throughout the rest of the year. Learning about the Ignatian approach to Scripture in a Lenten Bible study, for example, may open up a whole new way of reading the Bible and incorporating the meaning of its stories into your life. Experiencing contemplative prayer in a centering prayer group may be the beginning of a deeper life of prayer for you. Fasting on Ash Wednesday and Good Friday—perhaps for the first time—may introduce you to a connection between body and spirit that you have not made before. Many people find the practice of making a confession and meeting with a spiritual director during Lent essential to their spiritual health throughout the year.

Lent is a time to explore ways of growing in the Christian faith. To use the image of a spiritual journey again, Lent is a time to discover new spiritual paths and to return to those that have sustained you in the past. If you are new to the church, it might be useful to meet with one of the clergy or an experienced layperson in your congregation at the beginning of Lent to talk about what spiritual disciplines might be most helpful for you to undertake this year.

The Way of the Cross

This Lenten devotion began in the Holy Land in the custom of offering prayer at a series of places along the *Via Dolorosa* (Way of Sorrow)—those places traditionally associated with Jesus' suffering and death in Jerusalem. Prayers, readings, and reflections at these stations of the cross, as they are known, developed during the Crusades and spread to parishes throughout Christendom, and today we have a form of this devotion in our *Book of Occasional Services.* Many congregations offer the Way of the Cross on the Fridays in Lent, or at other appropriate times during the season.

The service is conducted with a number of stops (or "stations") throughout the church, cloister, or garden, each adorned with a wooden cross, icon, or other representation of the events being commemorated, from Jesus' condemnation by Pilate to his death on the cross.

A hymn is usually sung at the beginning of the service, and as participants move to each station. At each stop a brief paragraph is read describing the event being contemplated, followed by a prayer. In addition to participating in this service with others, many people find it helpful to follow the Way of the Cross as a private devotion during Lent.

ASH WEDNESDAY

The Lenten journey begins on Ash Wednesday, at a service held on the Wednesday before the first Sunday in Lent in which we have ashes smudged on our foreheads to remind us of our mortality and our need for forgiveness. We start here because we must know our need for mercy and grace before we can receive God's freely given gift of salvation. Some congregations hold early morning and noonday and evening services.

The practice of marking the foreheads of the faithful with ashes at the beginning of Lent seems to have originated in Gaul in the sixth century, when the beginning of the Lenten fast was moved from Sunday to the Wednesday before in order to make the season forty days long.[31] Dom Gregory Dix notes that the imposition of ashes was at first "confined to public penitents doing penance for grave and notorious sin, whom the clergy tried to comfort and encourage by submitting themselves to the same public humiliation."[32] It soon spread as a spiritual discipline for all those who wished to share in the Lenten fast before the Easter baptisms and to express publicly their penitence and desire for forgiveness.

The focus of Ash Wednesday is on penitence, or sorrow for sin, and fasting; the imposition of ashes is a reminder that we are mortal and that we receive eternal life as a free gift of God. At the appropriate time in the service you will be asked to come forward, and either stand or kneel. When the priest, deacon, or lay minister makes the sign of the cross with ashes on your forehead, he or she will say these sobering words: "Remember that you are dust, and to dust you shall return." Faced with the uncomfortable reality of human mortality, if our faith is to have any substance it is crucial that it can encompass even suffering and death, and thus be capable of seeing us through the passage to eternal life. Although on Ash Wednesday we are contemplating our mortality, we are also offering grateful thanks for our salvation in Jesus Christ, remembering that "it is only by [God's] gracious gift that we are given everlasting life" (BCP 265).

Today in our culture we do not readily grasp the symbolic significance of wearing the "sackcloth and ashes" referred to so

often in the Old Testament as a sign of repentance and mourning. In fact, most of the time when I have returned to work after
a noonday Ash Wednesday service my co-workers have simply
thought I had accidentally rubbed my forehead after reading an
inky newspaper at lunch or changing the toner in the copy
machine. (By the way, the ashes are not actually dirt, or ashes
from someone's fireplace. They are made by burning some of
the blessed palm fronds from the previous year's Palm Sunday
service.)

Whether you leave the ashes on your forehead after the service
or not is a matter of personal choice: some find it a helpful
reminder that this is a holy day in the church's calendar, and wish
to make a public witness to their faith. Others choose not to
announce their attendance at an Ash Wednesday liturgy publicly,
following Jesus' directive to "go into your room and shut the door
and pray to your Father who is in secret" (Matthew 6:6).

After the imposition of ashes the congregation reads or chants
Psalm 51 together, and then prays the Litany of Penitence. This
litany is a corporate, public confession of our failure to love "with
our whole heart, and mind, and strength," to serve "as Christ served
us," to forgive "as we have been forgiven." The priest or bishop then
pronounces the forgiveness we have been given by God.

Some people find it difficult to speak these words of confession and contrition. In our modern efforts toward "positive self
esteem" it can seem counterproductive to declare ourselves to be
miserable sinners. If we focus on our shortcomings, won't others
think less of us? Our common desire to appear better than we are,
to "put our best foot forward," can hinder us from even acknowl-
edging we *have* shortcomings. But Ash Wednesday is first and
foremost about honesty—coming clean by getting dirty, paradox-
ically speaking. The purpose of confession is not to feel "bad"
about yourself, but to be humbled in the sense of grounded in the
earth (*humus*), to be thoroughly human, to be cleansed from the
past to be free for the present and the future.

My ten-month-old son (if he could speak) would confess that
he is "only an infant" and thus does things now that hurt other

people. He hits his older brother with toys, he bites any finger that comes within inches of his teething gums, he complains loudly when he is disappointed or angry that he did not get his way. But we forgive all these offenses because our infinite love for him enables us to know that they do not represent who John is: they have to do with his development as a human being. In the months and years to come he will learn to use words instead of fists, to chew on toys instead of people, to be patient and less self-centered in controlling the events of his day.

In much the same way, on Ash Wednesday and throughout Lent we confess that we are "merely human"; we acknowledge our regret and sadness for those things we have done or left undone that have hurt ourselves and those around us. We confess our failure to live up to our baptismal vows. This is not to say that our failings are all developmental, or to deny the reality of sin so profound we call it evil: a quick glance at the daily newspaper reveals instances of human neglect, violence, and hatred. But as we confess our sins it is important to understand that we speak the words of penitence as a body—as a church and as a human race—rather than merely as individuals. We share in the sin of all because we are part of a fallen creation, alienated from God and from one another in deep and abiding ways.

At the conclusion of the Ash Wednesday service the celebrant offers a simple blessing of peace and forgiveness:

> Grant, most merciful Lord, to your faithful people pardon and peace, that they may be cleansed from all their sins, and serve you with a quiet mind. (*BOS* 25)

Before we leave Ash Wednesday, a quick word about Shrove Tuesday. On this day before Ash Wednesday many congregations offer a pancake supper, a tradition from the medieval custom of using up all the cream, eggs, and fat in the household before the Lenten fast. The word "shrove" comes from the verb "to shrive" (to confess and receive absolution), and refers to the practice of going to confession at the beginning of Lent. Another name you may hear for this day, especially in New Orleans, is "Mardi Gras," or Fat Tuesday.[33]

THE SUNDAY LITURGY IN LENT

When you arrive in church on the first Sunday in Lent you will notice the color of the vestments and altar hangings has changed from green (or whatever color your congregation uses for ordinary time) to either purple or some variation on unbleached linen—rough, flax-colored fabrics resembling sackcloth—bordered in one of the liturgical colors, called a "lenten array." Sometimes these vestments and altar hangings have symbols of Jesus' passion on them: a crown of thorns or a cross, perhaps. During Holy Week many congregations use matching veils to cover statues, crosses, and pictures and some follow the custom of veiling them throughout Lent. In some places, the altar is bare of its frontal during Lent.

You will probably also notice there are no flowers around the altar during Lent, or if there are they are subdued in color, size, and number. Many congregations put away their elaborate gold or brass candlesticks, processional crosses, and patens (plates) for the bread and chalices for the wine of the Eucharist during this season, using instead simple wooden crosses, candleholders made of wood, plain metal, or ceramic, and pewter or ceramic patens and chalices. Likewise, parishes usually do not celebrate weddings or baptisms during Lent unless there is an important reason to do so. The point is to remain in a simpler, quieter, more austere, penitential, and reflective stance during these weeks, staying "grounded" in who we are—in the words of the Ash Wednesday liturgy, to "remember that you are dust, and to dust you shall return" (BCP 265).

The other change you will notice on Sundays in Lent is that we omit the word "Alleluia" wherever it appears in the service. For example, when the priest holds up the bread and wine of the Eucharist and says, "Christ our Passover is sacrificed for us," the people's response during Lent is simply, "Therefore let us keep the feast," without the concluding *"Alleluia!"*

The Penitential Order

During Lent, many congregations begin their Sunday services of the Holy Eucharist with the Penitential Order, which is found in the Book of Common Prayer just prior to Rite One and Rite Two of the Holy Eucharist (BCP 319, 351). This order can be used on its own, but when it is used in the Eucharist it moves the confession to the beginning of the service, thus providing a penitential introductory focus appropriate for Lent.

The Exhortation and the Decalogue are often included in the Penitential Order at various times during Lent. (You can find the Exhortation and the Decalogue just before the Penitential Order.) One parish I know uses the Exhortation on the first Sunday in Lent and the Decalogue on the following Sundays. Other parishes choose to use only one, or neither.

In the Exhortation we humbly admit our need to prepare to receive communion "with penitent hearts and living faith." The prayer recalls the institution of the Lord's Supper on the night before Jesus died and urges us to "examine [our] lives and conduct by the rule of God's commandments." Finally, the Exhortation calls us to "acknowledge [our] sins before Almighty God" and make whatever restitution is required, and then to "go and open [our] grief to a discreet and understanding priest" if we are in need of help in our preparations, in order to receive "the assurance of pardon, and the strengthening of [our] faith" (BCP 316–17).

The Decalogue, or the Ten Commandments, is found in Exodus 20:1–17, and is provided in both traditional and contemporary language in the prayer book. In Rite One, after each commandment is read the people respond, "Lord, have mercy upon us, and incline our hearts to keep this law." In Rite Two the response is simply, "Amen. Lord have mercy" (BCP 317–18, 350).

The Great Litany

Another option for beginning the services of Lent is the Great Litany, though most congregations use this weighty order of petitions and responses only for the first Sunday in Lent. This litany was the first rite published in English, compiled by Archbishop Thomas Cranmer in 1544 as a "special supplication" during Henry VIII's war with Scotland and France.[34] You will hear echoes of those troubled times in the words of the litany.

Ideally the Great Litany is sung in procession, with servers, choir, clergy, and indeed all the congregation moving through the church if there is room. If not, then the congregation generally kneels during the litany while the choir, servers, and clergy process or join in kneeling.

The Catechumenate

If your congregation has some form of the catechumenate, then you will probably see various liturgies and prayers included for the candidates during the Sundays in Lent. Normally the First Sunday in Lent is the time for candidates to be enrolled, signing their names in a large book or parish register and answering several questions, along with their sponsors, about their desire to be baptized or to reaffirm their baptismal vows. Prayers then follow for the candidates, asking that they "may use this Lenten season wisely, joining with us in acts of self-denial and in performing works of mercy" (*BOS* 124).

The Book of Occasional Services assumes that throughout the Sundays in Lent "both the candidates and sponsors are prayed for by name in the Prayers of the People" (*BOS* 126). It also provides various prayers and blessings to be used for those participating in the catechumenate during Lent, though they certainly apply to all of us who seek during Lent to deepen our faith and understand more fully the meaning of our baptism in Christ:

> Lord Christ, true Light who enlightens every one: Shine, we pray, in the hearts of these candidates, that they may clearly see the way that leads to life eternal, and may follow it without stumbling; for you yourself are the Way, O Christ, as you are the Truth and the Life. . . . (*BOS* 127)

The Lectionary

For some seasons and feast days, the readings for Years A, B, and C in the lectionary are fairly similar. During Lent, however, these readings vary considerably but follow certain themes, such as covenant, conversion, rebirth, and resurrected life. In each of the three years, educator Joseph Russell believes, "the Bible readings appointed for the five Sundays in Lent provide a short course in the meaning of baptism."[35] Indeed, as Russell further notes, the readings outline the process for conversion:

> First we turn away from evil and toward Jesus Christ (Lent 1 and 2). Then we look at what we thirst for in life and ask for the empowerment of the Holy Spirit (Lent 3 and 4). Then we put our whole life and trust in Christ, who leads us even through death into life (Lent 5).[36]

The lectionary readings in Lent help to illumine the significance of our baptism and our life in Christ, by teaching us who we are, where we have come from, and where we are going. During Lent we hear the pivotal stories of creation and fall, the calling of Abraham, the covenant with Noah, the giving of the law to Moses, and the keeping of the Passover. Through the prophets we hear of the exile and suffering of the people of Israel, their call to repentance and new life, and their hope of a Messiah. In the New Testament readings from the letters sent by the apostles to the early Christian communities, we learn of the struggles of the new church to live as disciples of the risen Christ, to become a "new creation" through God's grace. And in the Gospels we hear of Jesus' temptation in the desert wilderness, his teachings and parables, his cleansing of the temple, and his call to his disciples to "take up their cross and follow me." Thus in all three years the readings contain the baptismal themes of conversion and repentance, death and new life, discipleship and vocation.

The Prayer over the People

Instead of the usual blessing at the end of the Eucharist, during Lent you may hear the celebrant say a solemn blessing called a "Prayer over the People" found in *The Book of Occasional Services*. The deacon or celebrant introduces the prayer with the words "Bow down before the Lord," and the congregation either bows low from the waist or kneels. The celebrant then offers the prayer given for that particular Sunday in Lent. For Lent 4, for example, the prayer is:

> Look down in mercy, Lord, on your people who kneel before you; and grant that those whom you have nourished by your Word and Sacraments may bring forth fruit worthy of repentance; through Christ our Lord. Amen. (*BOS* 25)

THE WEEKDAYS OF LENT

Lesser Feasts and Fasts includes proper collects, lessons, and psalms for the Eucharist on each of the weekdays of Lent, and many people choose to attend one or more weekday services as part of their Lenten discipline. Even if your church does not offer a daily Eucharist, these lessons and prayers can be the center of your daily devotions at home. The collect for Wednesday in the Fifth Week of Lent sums up our desire for true conversion of life as we enter the week of holy days before Easter:

> Almighty God our heavenly Father, renew in us the gifts of your mercy; increase our faith, strengthen our hope, enlighten our understanding, widen our charity, and make us ready to serve you.[37]

Keeping a spiritual discipline that includes regular prayer and the reading of Scripture throughout the weekdays of Lent will make these weeks of preparation for Easter more meaningful. You may also find that the ways you "keep a holy Lent" lay a sturdy foundation on which you can build throughout the rest of the year, as you grow in the Christian faith.

QUESTIONS FOR FURTHER THOUGHT AND DISCUSSION

1. What Lenten traditions do you remember from your childhood, if any? How has your understanding of Lent changed over time?

2. What Lenten disciplines have you or members of your family undertaken in recent years, if any? Are there different or additional spiritual disciplines you are considering for next Lent?

3. The early church developed the catechumenate as a way of preparing candidates for baptism. What topics do you think need to be discussed in baptismal preparation classes today?

4. Ash Wednesday is a difficult service for many people, who find it sobering to reflect on human mortality. Why do you think the church begins Lent in this way? Do you find the service a helpful way to start the Lenten season? Why or why not?

5. Read and reflect on the various Prayers over the People for Lent found in *The Book of Occasional Services,* pages 25 and 26. What Lenten themes do you hear?

Holy Week

*Almighty and everliving God, in your tender love for the human
race you sent your Son our Savior Jesus Christ to take upon
him our nature, and to suffer death upon the cross, giving us the
example of his great humility: Mercifully grant that we may walk
in the way of his suffering, and also share in his resurrection.*

Collect for Palm Sunday (BCP 219)

Holy Week is the last week in Lent, but the days of this week are
so important in the Christian calendar they merit their own chapter. The theme of Holy Week is Jesus' passion: his suffering and
death on the cross for our salvation. It can thus seem to be a rather
grim week, especially in those congregations whose piety reflects
the more medieval focus on Jesus' suffering—the blood he shed
and the physical, emotional, and spiritual anguish he endured.

Those who do not like to focus on such things might be
tempted to skip Holy Week, and move directly into Easter. It can
also be rather intimidating to see the calendar of services for this
week. Going to church every Sunday is quite a commitment for
many families with their busy schedules, and the prospect of
going on Wednesday, Thursday, Friday, and Saturday as well can
seem overwhelming. But the rites of Holy Week are at the very

heart of the Christian year, indeed of our Christian faith. And for many of us they are, year after year, the most meaningful and life-changing services of the church. You will not regret making room in your calendar for at least some, if not all, of these liturgies.

As on Ash Wednesday, it is vital to keep a broad perspective during this week. We walk through the days of Jesus' suffering and death because we believe they had a purpose—the salvation of the world. We believe Jesus' death conquered death itself for us all: that is the only reason why the Friday on which he died can be called "good." Even while we are sobered by the solemn reading of the gospel stories describing Jesus' death and deeply saddened by the ongoing violence in our world, from that day in Jerusalem to this Good Friday, we hold on to the faith that in Jesus God has brought about a new creation, and death itself has been conquered. "We have been buried with him by baptism into death," wrote the apostle Paul soon after Jesus' death, "so that, just as Christ was raised from the dead by the glory of the Father, so we too might walk in newness of life" (Romans 6:4).

HOLY WEEK IN THE EARLY CHURCH

Although the origins for Lent are a couple of centuries older, the rites of this week seem to have originated in Jerusalem in the fourth century during the time when Cyril of Jerusalem was bishop of the church there. As pilgrims poured into Jerusalem to celebrate their Easter baptisms, Cyril began leading them to the holy sites connected with the days leading up to Jesus' death. Joseph Russell describes the link to baptism in the early developments in the services of Holy Week in this way:

> With prayer, a dramatic reading of the story associated with the place, the singing of hymns, and symbolic actions, these events were experienced again by the pilgrims. By the time of their baptism, Paul's powerful words of dying in order to have new life could be appreciated. They were truly raised with Christ, they felt, because they had walked through his death in their baptism.[38]

It had long been the custom for the church to honor "local saints" by prayer at the site of their martyrdom or death, and in a sense the rites of Holy Week are part of that tradition. The homes where Jesus rested with his friends in nearby Bethany and ate his last supper with his disciples, the places where Jesus was tried by the Romans, where he died on the cross, where he was buried— all became sites of pilgrimage and honor among the early Christians. The emperor Constantine built churches on a number of these sites, and they offered a place of prayer for pilgrims during the week before Easter.

Most of what we know about the origins of Holy Week comes from the diary of a pilgrim named Egeria, the nun who visited Jerusalem in 385 and wrote her observations of this novel celebration of Holy Week in a diary for her sisters in Spain. Pilgrims like Egeria took these rites home with them, adapting them to their local needs and incorporating them into the liturgical services they kept each year.

From Egeria's diary we learn that on the Sunday that marks the beginning of Holy Week, "which they call here the Great Week," everyone gathered at the Martyrium, the church located on Golgotha, where they believed Jesus died on the cross. After celebrating a service there, they moved to the church on the Mount of Olives, "where the grotto in which the Lord taught is located."

The bishop sits down, hymns and antiphons appropriate to the day and place are sung, and there are likewise readings from the Scriptures. As the ninth hour approaches, they move up, chanting hymns, to the Imbomon, that is, to the place from which the Lord ascended into heaven; and everyone sits down there. . . . And there hymns and antiphons proper to the day and place are sung, interspersed with appropriate readings from the Scriptures and prayers.

Several hours later the passage from the gospel telling of Jesus' entry into Jerusalem is read. At that point, Egeria tells us, the bishop and all the people rise immediately, and then everyone walks down from the top of the Mount of Olives, with the people preceding the bishop and responding continually with "Blessed is He who comes in the name of the Lord" to the hymns and antiphons. . . . And the bishop is led in the same manner as the Lord once was led.[39]

The people made evening visits to the Mount of Olives on each of the first three days of Holy Week, Egeria continues, just as Jesus withdrew to the home of his friends in Bethany. On Maundy Thursday, the people celebrated the Eucharist in the Chapel of the Cross on the Mount of Olives rather than in the Martyrium at Golgotha, and a vigil was held. They visited Gethsemane after midnight and then returned to the city on the morning of Good Friday for the reading of the gospel passage describing the trial of Jesus. On that day they venerated the relics of the cross:

> The bishop sits on the throne, a table covered with a linen cloth is set before the bishop, and the deacons stand around the table. The gilded silver casket containing the sacred wood of the cross is brought in and opened. . . . It is the practice here for all the people to come forth one by one, the faithful as well as the catechumens, to bow down before the table, kiss the holy wood, and then move on.[40]

From noon until three o'clock a watch was held outdoors on the actual site of Golgotha, "regardless of whether it is raining or whether it is hot," with appropriate readings from the psalms, the letters, the Acts of the Apostles, and the gospels, and many prayers. Egeria notes that "it is astonishing how much emotion and groaning there is from all the people." Finally, in the evening there was a final visit to the Holy Sepulchre, where the gospel passage telling of the placing of Jesus' body in the tomb was read. Some remained to keep vigil there until the Easter Vigil took place on Saturday evening.

The liturgical scholar Dom Gregory Dix comments that "the intention of all this is obvious enough": visiting the sacred sites where Jesus lived and died naturally evoked in his followers feelings of anguished remorse for their sins and grateful joy in their experience of redemption. However, in the fourth century the church shifted from celebrating Easter as a single feast that included both Jesus' death and resurrection and that focused on the *theological* significance of these events to a series of liturgies that followed the *historical* events of Jesus' last week. To quote Marianne Micks again, as the "tourist's view of time"[41] increasingly predominated, Holy Week became a time in which Christians focused on walking the "way of the cross" with Jesus, from Palm Sunday through Maundy Thursday and Good Friday to Holy Saturday. The rites in Jerusalem were imitated and adapted far and wide, as "the way they do it in Jerusalem" became the "correct" way to keep Holy Week everywhere.[42]

HOLY WEEK IN THE EPISCOPAL CHURCH TODAY

Many centuries later, we, too, have become the beneficiaries of the Holy Week liturgies and traditions of Cyril's Jerusalem church, expanded and altered by Christians in the Middle Ages and Reformation and now once again adapted for modern Episcopalians. In the Middle Ages the church incorporated new ideas brought by the Crusaders (including the Stations of the Cross we described in the chapter on Lent) and embellished the liturgies with the more dramatic and emotive flavor of medieval piety. Crosses adorned with a symbolic figure of Christ the King became crucifixes portraying the broken and bloody body of Jesus.

During the twentieth century's liturgical movement the earlier rites from Jerusalem were recovered in the Episcopal Church, and their use gradually became more widespread in parishes. The Holy Week liturgies included in the 1979 Book of Common Prayer are in general closer to the classic commemorations at Jerusalem than their medieval offspring, though you will find a wide variety of devotional practices and "flavors" in the Episcopal Church. Anglo-Catholic parishes will tend to include more of the devotional traditions from the Middle Ages, while Evangelical parishes will tend to minimize those ritualistic dimensions of the services. Most Episcopal churches will fall somewhere in between.

The liturgical color for Holy Week is red, though it is not the bright red of Pentecost or ordinations but a more sober oxblood red or crimson, often decorated with black or off-white symbols. Some churches will continue to use their altar hangings for Lent, especially if they are of unbleached muslin rather than purple, so they do not clash with the dark red vestments.

You may hear a new word at this time of the year: the Triduum. You will not find it in the prayer book or the Bible, but it is a fairly common term among Episcopalians. *Triduum* is a Latin word meaning "three days," and it refers to the period of time beginning at sundown on Maundy Thursday through Good Friday and Holy Saturday to sundown on Easter. It thus corresponds to the early church's celebration of Easter, with two days of fasting and one of feasting, and includes the liturgies for Maundy Thursday, Good Friday, Holy Saturday, the Easter Vigil, and all the services on Easter.

In our prayer book today you will find in the Proper Liturgies for Special Days section, after the liturgy for Ash Wednesday, all the primary liturgies of Holy Week: Palm Sunday, Maundy Thursday, Good Friday, and Holy Saturday (BCP 270–83). *The Book of Occasional Services* provides additional rites for other services you often encounter during this week: The Way of the Cross (familiarly known as the Stations of the Cross), Tenebrae, the rite for the footwashing on Maundy Thursday, and an Agapé fellowship supper for Maundy Thursday (*BOS* 57–96). In cathedrals and large congregations you will notice a multitude of services, choral concerts, and perhaps even passion plays during Holy Week; yet even very small churches can offer simple, solemn, and beautiful services for each of the days of this week.

For those congregations with an active catechumenate, the days of Holy Week are a special time of preparation for baptism at Easter. The candidates for baptism and those who are reaffirming

their baptismal vows are generally included in each of the services in meaningful ways, from participating in the washing of
feet on Maundy Thursday to reading the lessons at the Easter
Vigil.

Finally, a word about the emotional effect of these services. If
you have not entered into the liturgies of Holy Week before,
you may be surprised to find that they can evoke powerful emo-
tions. Though in our reserved American churches today you
will probably not hear the "groaning" that the pilgrim Egeria
describes on Good Friday, the services of Holy Week deal with
subjects that can touch us deeply. During this week we focus
on the suffering and death of the innocent and vulnerable, the
failure to stand by someone in need, and wrenching farewell
conversations at a final meal with beloved friends. We also
ponder moments of injustice, cruelty, and arrogant "hardness of
heart"—experiences that we know all too well in our own
world. These events in Jesus' life are human events, common to
all of us who have endured the loss or betrayal of loved ones or
the bitterness of unjust treatment to or from others. The rites
commemorating these days at the end of Jesus' life may well call
to our remembrance the feelings of sorrow, anger, fear, sadness,
loneliness, and remorse we knew at those times in our lives.
This ability to touch our emotional core is part of the power of
Holy Week. Many of us have found that experiencing the emotional weight of these services can be a path of healing as well as
of deeper understanding, especially when our concerns are shared
with a trusted friend or priest.

PALM SUNDAY

The full name given in the 1979 prayer book for this day is
The Sunday of the Passion: Palm Sunday. These two traditional
names reveal the dual focus of this day: Jesus' suffering and
death on the Friday of Passover, and his triumphal entry into
Jerusalem only a few days before. The liturgy is a combination
of several ancient rites that would have been done over the
course of many hours. So condensing these two very different

commemorations into a single one-hour service can be difficult to do well. Sometimes as this service moves along we are not sure if we should be celebrating or mourning—or both! So it is important to notice the clear distinction between the Liturgy of the Palms and the Sunday of the Passion within the service.

The Liturgy of the Palms

The Liturgy of the Palms usually begins with a procession with palms, so you may wish to arrive a few minutes early for this service. Sometimes the procession starts outdoors in a garden or space near the church; in inclement weather it might be in the parish hall or another large meeting room in the church building. It can also begin in the back of the worship space, with the procession moving along the aisles.

After the opening prayer, the deacon or priest reads one of the gospel passages describing Jesus' entry into Jerusalem riding on a donkey as the people, spreading palm branches on the road before him, joyfully acclaimed him as a prophet of God, shouting, "Hosanna to the Son of David! Blessed is the one who comes in the name of the Lord!" (Matthew 21:8–9).

After the reading of the gospel the priest or bishop will bless the palm branches to be used in the procession. Most congregations today use the palm fronds available from church supply houses, but the prayer book actually encourages the earlier custom of using the freshly cut branches of local trees and shrubs, even supplemented by flowers. As Dom Gregory Dix notes, the single strands of palm fronds we have now, like the small crosses many congregations like to fold them into, "can hardly be waved and certainly fail to signify a parade."[43]

After the deacon dismisses the people the procession begins, led by the crucifer, acolytes, altar party, and choir, into the church's worship space. A traditional hymn for the procession is "All glory, laud, and honor." The text, written in the late eighth or early ninth century, describes the historical entry into Jerusalem while linking that first procession to our ongoing and present celebration of the coming of Jesus "in the Lord's name."

Thou art the King of Israel, thou David's royal Son,
who in the Lord's Name comest, the King and Blessed One.

The company of angels is praising thee on high;
and we with all creation in chorus make reply.

The people of the Hebrews with palms before thee went;
our praise and prayers and anthems before thee we present.[44]

Another traditional hymn associated with the procession is a
portion of Psalm 118 set to plainchant,[45] part of which is quoted in
the gospel reading for the day: "Blessed is he who comes in the name
of the Lord," interpreted by the early Christians as referring to Jesus.

The Sunday of the Passion
After the procession, the tone and focus of the service changes
distinctly, from the joyful celebration of Jesus' triumphal entry to
the sorrowful remembrance of his passion. The palm fronds are
put away as we listen to the Scripture readings for the Sunday of
the Passion, including the passion gospel. This extended reading
from Matthew, Mark, or Luke tells the story of Jesus' prayer in the
garden of Gethsemane, his trial and torture at the hands of the
Romans, his crucifixion and death on the cross, and his burial. It
may seem premature to read this gospel now, before Maundy
Thursday and Good Friday, but the tradition of reading the story
of the passion on this Sunday developed before the liturgies of
Holy Week. Originally the different versions of the passion story
in the four gospels were read on each of the days before Good
Friday; in our current lectionary the church has adapted that tradition by assigning Matthew, Mark, and Luke to be read on Palm
Sunday in Years A, B, and C, and reading the passion gospel from
John on Good Friday. In a culture that is increasingly secular and
diverse in its religious faiths, so that many people are now
required to work or attend school on Good Friday, it may be helpful for those who cannot attend services during the week to hear
the passion gospel on this Sunday before Easter.

Other readings for the Sunday of the Passion include one of the familiar readings from Isaiah telling of the Suffering Servant:

Surely he has borne our infirmities
  and carried our diseases;
yet we accounted him stricken,
  struck down by God, and afflicted.
But he was wounded for our transgressions,
  crushed for our iniquities;
upon him was the punishment that made us whole,
  and by his bruises we are healed. (Isaiah 53:4–5)

The psalm for this portion of the liturgy is Psalm 22, with its plaintive cry, "My God, my God, why have you forsaken me?"— so different from the "I will give thanks to you, for you answered me and have become my salvation" of Psalm 118, read earlier in the service. The reading from Paul's letter to the Philippians likewise speaks of Jesus' death, and may be part of a very early church poem or hymn:

And being found in human form,
  he humbled himself
and became obedient to the point of death—
  even death on a cross. (Philippians 2:7–8)

The passion gospel was traditionally sung by three deacons, but most congregations today no longer have such an abundance of deacons so a number of alternative approaches have developed. In many places the passion gospel is a dramatic presentation narrated by the deacon or priest, with various members of the congregation taking on the speaking parts throughout the narrative—Peter, Jesus, the centurion, the servant girl, Caiaphas, and so on. Congregations with a strong choral tradition may sing the passion gospel, with a number of voices or only two or three. The congregation as a whole speaks (or sings) the parts of the crowd, which includes the cry "Crucify him!"; many people understandably find shouting these words aloud difficult, but participating in this way brings home the horror of Jesus' execution. The normal responses to the gospel ("Praise to you, Lord Christ") are omitted on this Sunday, and the silence again emphasizes the solemnity of this day.

After the passion gospel the Eucharist continues as usual during Lent, though the Nicene Creed and confession may be omitted. The service may conclude with the Prayer over the People for Palm Sunday through Maundy Thursday, a prayer you will also hear at the beginning of the liturgy for Good Friday:

> Almighty God, we pray you graciously to behold this your family, for whom our Lord Jesus Christ was willing to be betrayed, and given into the hands of sinners, and to suffer death upon the cross. (*BOS 26*)

MONDAY, TUESDAY, AND WEDNESDAY IN HOLY WEEK

The only special liturgical provisions for the first three weekdays of Holy Week are the lessons and collects given in the prayer book, which your parish will use for services on these days if its custom is to schedule daily Morning or Evening Prayer or weekday Eucharists. The gospel readings tell of the events during those days between Jesus' arrival in Jerusalem and the final supper he shared with his friends on Thursday evening.

In these stories we learn that early in the week, while Jesus stayed with his friends in Bethany, a woman anointed Jesus' feet with costly perfume in preparation for his burial. He visited the temple in Jerusalem and drove out the people who were selling the animals required for sacrifice and who exchanged common currency for temple money, thus exploiting the poor and all those who came to worship in the process. He continued to teach his disciples during that final week, telling them, "I have come as light into the world, so that everyone who believes in me should not remain in the darkness" (John 12:46). Finally, on Thursday he was betrayed to the Jewish authorities by one of his own disciples, Judas, for thirty pieces of silver.

Even if your parish does not offer services on the Monday, Tuesday, and Wednesday of Holy Week, you can read the lessons and prayers provided for these days at home. Also, in many places you will find the service of Tenebrae offered on one of these early weekdays of Holy Week, most often on Wednesday evening.

Tenebrae

The word *tenebrae* comes from the Latin for "darkness" or "shadows," and the hauntingly beautiful liturgy for Tenebrae found in our *Book of Occasional Services* is a compilation of the three ancient monastic night and early morning offices (services of prayer and Scripture readings) of the last three days of Holy Week. In the Middle Ages the church kept these offices on Wednesday, Thursday, and Friday evenings, but the form we have now is to be used on Wednesday only so that "the proper liturgies of Maundy Thursday and Good Friday may find their places as the principal services of those days" (*BOS* 74).

If you have never attended a Tenebrae service, make plans to do so this year: as *The Book of Occasional Services* describes it, Tenebrae is a deeply moving "extended meditation upon, and a prelude to, the events in our Lord's life between the Last Supper and the Resurrection" (*BOS* 74). The two prominent features of this service are the chanting of portions of the biblical book of Lamentations and the gradual extinguishing of fourteen candles and all the other lights in the church until only a single candle, symbolizing the Lord, remains in the darkness.

When you arrive in the evening for this service you will see fifteen candles lighted. The service consists of the reading of a number of psalms, prayers, and canticles. The readings from Lamentations are divided into paragraphs, each beginning with a letter of the Hebrew alphabet, and the traditional chant for these readings is deeply resonant and reflective of the church's Jewish and medieval roots. A candle is extinguished at the end of each psalm, and by the end of the service the church is in darkness. After praying the collect, a loud sound is made in the darkness, symbolizing the earthquake at the resurrection, and the people leave in silence.

MAUNDY THURSDAY

As you arrive for the Eucharist on Maundy Thursday, instead of the customary morning sunlight streaming through the stained-glass windows you may find only the muted glow of the evening's gathering darkness. The altar candles are lit for the service, and the altar frontal is the oxblood red of Holy Week, or perhaps a subdued white. A large pitcher of water and a stack of towels sit beside a wide-mouthed bowl to the side of the altar. Those who have already gathered in the pews are quieter than usual, some sitting alone in reflection and anticipation.

The name Maundy Thursday comes from the Latin *mandatum,* the root of our English word "mandate" or "command." It refers to the new commandment to "love one another" (John 13:34) that Jesus gave his disciples, after he had washed their feet on the Thursday of his final week in Jerusalem. Over the millennia a number of rites and meanings have been associated with Maundy Thursday: it is also the day when the oils used in baptism and other sacraments are blessed, when those who have been separated from the church for some reason confess their sins and reconcile with God and the community, and when bishops, priests, and deacons reaffirm the vows they made when they were ordained. Maundy Thursday is also the day when the consecrated bread and wine of the Eucharist are reserved, or set aside, for communion on Good Friday.

But Maundy Thursday is perhaps best known as our commemoration of the meal at which Jesus instituted the Eucharist, or Holy Communion, on the night before he died, and for the washing of his disciples' feet. Maundy Thursday is an evening of transition, as we move through Jesus' final evening with his disciples, beginning with the Passover meal, through his anguished prayer in the garden of Gethsemane, to his betrayal and arrest. The liturgy begins in the warmth of vesper glow and candlelight reflecting the rich colors of the altar cloths, and ends in the dark, the altar stripped and bare, the congregation leaving quietly or holding silent, prayerful vigil in a garden or side chapel.

The sudden reversals during this evening can be disconcerting. Is this an evening of celebrating the institution of the Lord's Supper, or a time to repent of the many occasions of our own betrayals of our Lord? Is this evening a call to serve others as Jesus served them by washing their feet, or a time to sense with prayerful foreboding the events of the Friday to come? Maundy Thursday is all of these things, and its multiple facets can add to the richness of the liturgy as we move through Jesus' final evening with his disciples and come to understand our own participation in the community of disciples—the church—in a deeper way.

One way to understand the significance of the series of events commemorated on Maundy Thursday is to see them as Jesus' final teachings to his beloved friends and companions. On this evening Jesus may remind us of a dying mother struggling to say goodbye to her children. She may write them letters of instruction for the future, perhaps urging them to love their brothers and sisters. She may remind them of the family rituals through which they have shared deep moments of intimacy, and tell them that each time they do those things after she has gone—enjoy meals around the kitchen table, celebrate family birthdays, take walks together in the woods, read books aloud before bedtime—they will experience her presence with them yet again. In much the same way, in the washing of the disciples' feet and the institution of the Eucharist, Jesus is telling his beloved children—the church—how and where they will experience his presence after his physical body is no longer with them. They will find him in the breaking of the bread and sharing of the wine of the Eucharist, and in serving one another in love.

The Lessons

The collect for Maundy Thursday lays out the themes of this evening:

Almighty Father, whose dear Son, on the night before he suffered, instituted the Sacrament of his Body and Blood: Mercifully grant

*that we may receive it thankfully in remembrance of Jesus Christ
our Lord, who in these holy mysteries gives us a pledge of eternal
life.* (BCP 274)

The Scripture lessons provided for Maundy Thursday likewise
concentrate on the Eucharist. The reading from Exodus tells the
story of the first Passover kept by the Hebrew people while they
were slaves in Egypt. We read this lesson from Exodus tonight
because of the connection Christians make between the keeping
of Passover and our belief in Jesus as the Lamb of God, whose
blood takes away the sin of the world. The Last Supper that Jesus
shared with his friends was either a Passover meal (as in the gospel
accounts of Matthew, Mark, and Luke) or a meal that took place
twenty-four hours before the Passover (as in the gospel account of
John). In either case, the Last Supper was surrounded by Passover
associations that provided the background to its meaning and the
foundation for later interpretation by the early Christians. For the
Israelites, the Passover feast was not simply a memorial of a past
event, but a feast of deliverance and redemption experienced *now.*
In the same way, the Last Supper for Christians became a means
through which Christ's real presence was experienced in the bread
and wine of communion in the present moment, in every community through the ages.

In the reading from the first letter to the Corinthians, Paul
relates the account of the Last Supper that he received "from the
Lord" (1 Corinthians 11:23). Since Paul's letters were largely written before the gospels, this account represents the earliest tradition
we have of Jesus' words and actions on his last evening with his
disciples. These verses have become very familiar to most Episcopalians—indeed, most Christians—as they are quoted every Sunday in the Eucharist as the priest consecrates the bread and wine:

*On the night he was handed over to suffering and death, our Lord
Jesus Christ took bread; and when he had given thanks to you, he
broke it, and gave it to his disciples, and said, "Take, eat: This is my
Body, which is given for you. Do this for the remembrance of me."*

> *After supper he took the cup of wine; and when he had given thanks, he gave it to them, and said, "Drink this, all of you: This is my Blood of the new Covenant, which is shed for you and for many for the forgiveness of sins. Whenever you drink it, do this for the remembrance of me."* (BCP 362–63; see also 1 Corinthians 11:23–25)

The account of the Last Supper we hear tonight from Luke's gospel is similar to Paul's, except that it is more clearly linked to the setting of the Passover meal. In it, Jesus and his friends drink from a common cup before Jesus breaks the bread and blesses the wine. Some scholars have suggested that the common cup refers to a practice in which the person presiding at Jewish meals would pass his own cup to someone singled out for the special honor of sharing in the blessing said over that cup. In sharing his cup with all of his disciples, Jesus thus reiterates the message he sent when he washed their feet: as his body, the church, they are to share equally in the blessings of participation in a community grounded in love and service.

An alternative gospel reading describes the story of Jesus washing the disciples' feet. Some congregations choose to alternate the gospel readings each year; others read the footwashing story only on those years when the footwashing is part of the liturgy.

> *And during supper Jesus, knowing that the Father had given all things into his hands, and that he had come from God and was going to God, got up from the table, took off his outer robe, and tied a towel around himself. Then he poured water into a basin and began to wash the disciples' feet and to wipe them with the towel that was tied around him.* (John 13:2–5)

After Jesus has finished washing the feet of each disciple, he returned to the table and asked them, "Do you know what I have done to you?" Luke does not record their response, if indeed they had one. So Jesus answered for them:

You call me Teacher and Lord—and you are right, for that is
what I am. So if I, your Lord and Teacher, have washed your
feet, you also ought to wash one another's feet. For I have set you
an example, that you also should do as I have done to you.
(John 13:13–15)

In the same way, we in the church continue to wash one another's
feet as a sign of our willingness to learn what it means to love as
Jesus loves.

The Footwashing

After the sermon the celebrant gathers the waiting towel and
basin and invites the congregation to come forward to have their
feet washed, remembering Jesus' example. If this is your first
experience of Maundy Thursday you may be wondering—perhaps curiously, perhaps a bit uneasily—what will happen next. It
is a moment in the liturgy that many people cherish and others
dread.

Not every congregation chooses to include the footwashing in
the Maundy Thursday service, and for a variety of reasons. Of all
the liturgies of the church, the footwashing is perhaps the most
awkward for modern Christians. Some congregations have elected
to focus rather on the institution of the Eucharist and omit this
liturgy altogether or just hear its message in the gospel reading.

In first-century Palestine, where the sandy, dusty roads were
rarely paved, almost everyone wore sandals. Guests would arrive
at the door with gritty feet in need of washing, and it was simple
common courtesy to be greeted by someone—often a slave—
with a basin of water and a towel waiting. Jesus refers to this custom when a woman anoints his feet with costly ointment while
he dines in the home of Simon the Pharisee:

Turning toward the woman, he said to Simon, "Do you see this
woman? I entered your house; you gave me no water for my feet,
but she has bathed my feet with her tears and dried them with
her hair." (Luke 7:44)

For Jesus and his disciples, removing their sandals and washing their feet was something they did in public daily—probably several times a day. Today we prefer to tend to our bathing needs in private: only the very young, the very old, and the very sick are bathed by others, and in our appearance-conscious culture we are especially private about our well-worn, sometimes smelly, often sweaty feet. Removing our shoes and socks and placing our bare feet into the hands of a fellow Christian is an embarrassingly intimate gesture for us, rather than the matter of simple, useful, attentive service it was in the time of Jesus.

So it is logical to question the meaning and value of this ritual today, especially in congregations where very few people wish to come forward at the time of the invitation. "What does the footwashing ceremony have to say to us now?" is a legitimate question to ask. And yet for many people the washing of feet continues to be an act filled with powerful spiritual significance. Those who have pushed themselves through the cultural barrier and have risked placing their feet in the hands of a fellow Christian, or who have taken up towel and basin to wash the feet of others, testify to the power this ritual has to teach us about Christian love and service in the midst of a real, flesh-and-blood community. For many of us the church is a place in which the cultural and personal boundaries separating us from one another are broken down, as healing and trust replace brokenness and guarded self-protection. Fellow Christians become family, and the intimacy of the footwashing is simply another way of expressing that ease and familiarity in a liturgical act.

Perhaps the better question for us to ask is "What can we learn from our embarrassment about the washing of feet?" It is important that we grasp and live out the fundamental teaching of Jesus to his disciples following the footwashing: those who teach, who lead, who have power are no better in God's eyes than those who work by serving the needs of others, who have no earthly power, who wash feet. On Maundy Thursday we are commanded to love one another as *Jesus loves us*—and that means in the kind of attentive service that is physical, practical, and in *this* world, not just in the next.

In parishes that struggle with how to ease the discomfort of this part of the service, sometimes several members of the congregation are asked to volunteer for the footwashing ahead of time. They can then arrive at the service prepared (for instance, it is better not to wear pantyhose that evening!) and can come forward to "break the ice," so to speak, encouraging others to follow their example. Sometimes only a representative number of parishioners—usually twelve, to symbolize the twelve apostles—have their feet washed. You should be able to tell from the invitation of the celebrant and the notes in the bulletin what the custom is in your parish.

Above all, it is important to relax and enjoy this part of the service. When we were visiting our new parish for the first time on Maundy Thursday one of the moments that told us this was the place for us was the footwashing. In the midst of a service that was gracefully done in classic Anglican style, with beautiful music and eloquent preaching, the footwashing was a moment that reminded us of our children's baths at home: cheerfully chaotic but full of love, with spilled water and large feet that did not quite fit into the small bowls, as well as lots of affectionate smiles and friendly hands to help people stand up again on their wonderfully clean feet.

The Reserved Sacrament

If you notice that at the offertory an extra flagon of wine and basket of bread are brought to the altar, you may wonder why. At least since the early fifth century, it has been customary not to celebrate the Eucharist on Good Friday, in remembrance of Jesus' crucifixion and death on that day—indeed, it is one of only two days in the church year on which the Eucharist may not be celebrated. (Holy Saturday, the day before Easter, is the other.) But because we still recognize Christ's abiding presence on that day, many congregations wish to include communion in their Good Friday observances. In order to do so, they consecrate additional bread and wine on the evening of Maundy Thursday.

This reserved sacrament, as it is called, is usually kept in a place of reverence, often in a side chapel or area designated for a vigil of watching, waiting, and praying during the night.

The Lord's Supper

This evening's liturgy continues with one of the familiar prayers of consecration, which includes the passage recalling the words of institution of the Lord's Supper heard earlier in the Scripture lessons: "Take, eat: This is my Body, which is given for you. Do this for the remembrance of me. . . ." The words echo more profoundly this evening, jarred from their overfamiliar rhythm in this context of the night before Jesus' death on Good Friday. We can see Jesus at table with his disciples; we can feel the warm air in the room, see the flickering candlelight, smell the foods of the Passover, taste the bread and wine. We can sense the tension, the love, the fear, the impending grief of the disciples.

As you go forward to share in this evening's Supper of the Lord, you may be more aware than ever of the people near you as you walk up the aisle and perhaps kneel or stand at the altar rail or wait in line at one of the various stations for communion. The priest places the bread in your hands, soft and fragrant if it is freshly baked rather than a symbolic wafer; the wine is sweet and warming. On this night of the institution of the Lord's Supper you know yourself to be gathered into the community of disciples around the Lord.

The Stripping of the Altar

But after you have returned to your pew, you may notice the light from the tabernacle that is usually lit is no longer glowing, and the door stands open, revealing an empty space inside. The extra bread and wine that were consecrated are solemnly carried to a side chapel or other space nearby, where a simple "garden" may have been prepared for a vigil through the night. Kneeling, the congregation reads aloud Psalm 22 as the clergy, acolytes, and perhaps members of the altar guild or other parishioners silently remove all the ornaments of beauty in the sanctuary: the candles, the vestments, the cruets and patens and chalices, the processional cross, even the white altar linens.

Finally, the altar area is barren and dark. The warmth of the community sharing its communion fades in the gathering darkness. There is no dismissal tonight. Most of the congregation leaves in silence, though several people move slowly to sit in the place of vigil and kneel before the reserved sacrament, and you may choose to join them.

The Night Vigil

In many parishes, it is customary to hold a Maundy Thursday vigil of prayer throughout the night—or at least for several hours after the conclusion of the service. Usually people sign up to keep watch in pairs for a set period of time, perhaps thirty minutes or an hour. The vigil symbolizes our movement through Jesus' last night with his disciples, as he walked with them to the Mount of Olives to pray.

> *They went to a place called Gethsemane; and he said to his disciples, "Sit here while I pray." He took with him Peter and James and John, and began to be distressed and agitated. And he said to them, "I am deeply grieved, even to death; remain here, and keep awake."* (Mark 14:32–34)

Despite his intense suffering and his plea for companionship, Jesus finds the disciples sleeping as he prays—not once, but three times. The disciples' betrayal by their inability to stay awake with him is further deepened as the soldiers and Jewish leaders arrive to arrest him: one of their own number, the one who had shared Jesus' bread, has given him into their hands.

Here we experience the final reversal of Maundy Thursday. The disciples who felt his hands gently washing and drying their feet, who shared his last meal, who listened as he prayed and taught and loved them: these same disciples could not stay with him through his suffering. And as we sit in silent vigil, or make our way quietly home, our feet still fresh and clean and our mouths still tasting the bread and wine of communion, we know that we can be equally inadequate in our love—equally fickle, equally fearful and self-preserving.

And yet our human failings are not the final word. The events of Easter are that word; the redeeming love of God is the ultimate truth, not human sin. As you slip into a chair in the place of vigil, you pray beside others who are equally frail, equally fickle, equally fearful—and equally beloved. And so, held within the community of fellow disciples, we continue to move through this Holy Week, through the night of Maundy Thursday into the dawn of Good Friday.

GOOD FRIDAY

On Friday in Holy Week the church commemorates the crucifixion and death of Jesus. This is one of the days of the Triduum, and is among the most sober days of the church calendar. However, it is important to note that the Good Friday liturgy is *not* a funeral. Just as on Maundy Thursday we remember Jesus' institution of the Last Supper even as we celebrate the Eucharist week by week, so on Good Friday we remember Jesus' suffering and death while celebrating the victory over death he has won for us now. Although the liturgical color for Good Friday remains black in some places, most congregations have adopted the older tradition of using oxblood red for the vestments on this day.

Originally the days we call Good Friday and Easter were one event marking the death and resurrection of Jesus, a single fast on Friday and Saturday leading to the Easter Vigil on Saturday night. By the time of Egeria's travels, however, at least in Jerusalem the church had begun to separate the two days with special rites on Good Friday, and over the next millennia a wide variety of observances developed around this day. What we have in our prayer book now is a compilation of a number of these rites, and you may find that your parish adds other traditions as well, depending on its local customs.

When you arrive in church today—which may be at twelve noon, or in the evening if most of the people in your congregation cannot attend a service during the workday—the altar and the space around it will still be bare. The reserved sacrament will have remained in the place of vigil during the night. Silence is usually kept before this service, and the clergy and lay ministers enter in silence. In fact, I have found this is the most difficult service to bring my children to because of the sober message of the liturgy and the profound silence surrounding the devotions on this day, and I am always grateful when a congregation offers a special service for children and families.

You may be familiar with other services different Christian denominations have developed over the centuries, perhaps called the Seven Last Words, or the Three Hours. Often held from noon to three o'clock, the hours when Jesus hung on the cross, these services tend to include readings from the passion gospel or other devotional writings, prayers, hymns, and homilies or meditations interspersed among periods of silence. You will increasingly find ecumenical services on Good Friday. Praying with Christians from other denominations on this holy day can be an important way to realize the fundamental unity of the church despite our many differences.

In our prayer book there are three parts to the Good Friday liturgy. The first is a very simple Liturgy of the Word, in which we hear once again the passion gospel, as well as readings from the Old and New Testaments. We then pray a series of intercessions and prayers called the Solemn Collects. The second part of the service is the Veneration of the Cross, which is either a simple honoring of the cross or an elaborate ritual, depending on the customs in your parish. Finally, in most places the service concludes with communion from the reserved sacrament.

The Lessons

The readings assigned for today all focus on sacrifice, suffering, and death—heavy, sometimes problematic yet important aspects of Christian theology, with their roots deeply embedded in Judaism. The story in Genesis of Abraham's journey up the mountain to sacrifice his son Isaac as a burnt offering raises many questions for us about what kind of God would call Abraham to do something we consider so horrific. In Isaiah we also see the image of the sacrificial lamb:

> *All we like sheep have gone astray;*
>   *we have all turned to our own way,*
> *and the LORD has laid on him*
>   *the iniquity of us all.* (Isaiah 53:6)

And in the letter to the Hebrews we hear of the "perfect offering" of Jesus' body that has done away with animal sacrifices:

> *Since we have confidence to enter the sanctuary by the blood of Jesus, by the new and living way that he opened for us through the curtain (that is, through his flesh), and since we have a great priest over the house of God, let us approach with a true heart in full assurance of faith, with our hearts sprinkled clean from an evil conscience and our bodies washed with pure water.*
> (Hebrews 10:19–22)

The concept of a blood sacrifice for sin is foreign to many of us today, and although it is part of the church's complex theology of redemption, it is not the whole of that theology. If you have questions about this interpretation of the meaning of Jesus' death, you will not find all the answers during this service, so it is important to continue to study, learn, listen, ask, and explore in the coming weeks.

The passion gospel read today is from John, and as on Palm Sunday it is usually done by several people as a dramatic presentation, either spoken or sung, and narrated by the deacon or priest, or by a member of the congregation.

The Solemn Collects

In this ancient form of intercessory prayer the deacon reads the part called the "biddings" ("Let us pray for . . .") and the celebrant reads the prayers—called "collects"—that conclude the intercessions. We pray for the church, for all nations and governments, for people who are in need, for those who "have not received the Gospel of Christ," and "for the grace of a holy life" until we "enter into the fullness of the joy of our Lord, and receive the crown of life in the day of resurrection" (BCP 279–80).

Some churches conclude the Good Friday liturgy at this point, after singing a hymn and praying a concluding prayer. In other places, the liturgy continues with either the veneration of the cross or communion from the reserved sacrament, or both.

The Veneration of the Cross

At this point the prayer book is rather vague about what will happen next, saying only that after a wooden cross is brought into the church "appropriate devotions may follow." This is one of the times you will see the broad diversity of worship styles within the Episcopal Church in action. Some congregations will ask the people to kneel in their pews at this point while the anthems, restored from their medieval liturgies in the 1979 prayer book, are recited or sung. Others will invite (though never require) you to walk up the aisle to touch, kiss, or bow to a large cross that is held there for veneration, with elaborate choral anthems sung at this time. It all depends on how comfortable your congregation is with this more medieval and catholic piety.

We know from the pilgrim Egeria that Christians have been honoring the cross in this way for centuries. The church in Jerusalem believed it had a relic of the actual wooden cross on which Jesus died, and the practice of venerating the cross spread throughout the church as the pilgrims returned home. Egeria notes that occasionally there were excesses in devotion: "It is said that someone (I do not know when) took a bite and stole a piece of the holy cross," she wrote. "Therefore, it is now guarded by the deacons standing around, lest there be anyone who would dare come and do that again."[46] The veneration of the cross can seem an odd or even superstitious practice to many today, with our focus on more "spiritual" and "intellectual" worship, but many others find it important to honor Jesus' suffering and death in such a tangible, physical way. It takes courage to try something new, but sometimes you may be surprised to discover ways of worshiping that bring a different dimension and depth to your spiritual life. Like the rest of us, you will no doubt also find your own place of comfort within the spectrum of piety in the Episcopal Church as time goes on.

Communion from the Reserved Sacrament

Since by longstanding tradition there is no celebration of the Eucharist on Good Friday or Holy Saturday, if a congregation wishes to have communion on this day it must be from bread and wine consecrated at a previous Eucharist—usually the Maundy Thursday service. In contrast to the elaborate prayers and rites attached to a normal celebration of the Eucharist, this brief service of communion is very simple. After a confession of sin and the Lord's Prayer, you will be asked to come forward and receive the bread and wine. Then you will pray a rather sober concluding prayer that sums up the focus of Good Friday:

> *Lord Jesus Christ, Son of the living God, we pray you to set your passion, cross, and death between your judgment and our souls, now and in the hour of our death. Give mercy and grace to the living; pardon and rest to the dead; to your holy Church peace and concord; and to us sinners everlasting life and glory.* (BCP 282)

The people then depart in silence, with no blessing or dismissal given. Sometimes I find it difficult to "reenter" the noisy, bustling, seemingly frivolous world after spending several hours in silence and prayerful meditation on Jesus' suffering and death. One custom many of us have found helpful in making the transition is the tradition of sharing hot cross buns after the Good Friday liturgy. It is a gentle way to break one's fast, to return to our everyday lives, as it calmly reassures us that even in the midst of the heaviness of this day Easter is not far away. Even in the face of infinite human fear, pain, and anguish, we still believe with the fourteenth-century English anchorite Julian of Norwich that ultimately, in God's time and in God's way, "all shall be well, and all shall be well, and all manner of thing shall be well."

HOLY SATURDAY

On Holy Saturday we remember the burial of Jesus, and the time he spent among the dead. There is a simple liturgy of readings and prayers for this day, and if your congregation does not offer a service today it is helpful to read the lessons at home.

In one parish I know it is a tradition to spend time in the garden on this day, to get one's hands dirty in the *humus* of the earth and feel the warmth of the sun. This last day of Lent is a day for remembering the words spoken on Ash Wednesday at the beginning of Lent: "Remember that you are dust, and to dust you shall return."

For me, Holy Saturday is also a day for giving thanks for the friends who accompany us on our life journey to the very end. In John's gospel we read of Joseph of Arimathea and Nicodemus braving their fear of discovery and coming forward to care for Jesus' body after his death:

> *Joseph of Arimathea, who was a disciple of Jesus, though a secret*
> *one because of his fear of the Jews, asked Pilate to let him take*
> *away the body of Jesus. Pilate gave him permission; so he came*
> *and removed his body. Nicodemus, who had at first come to Jesus*
> *by night, also came, bringing a mixture of myrrh and aloes,*
> *weighing about a hundred pounds.* (John 19:38–39)

We all need friends and loved ones who will care for our bodies when we are infirm and after our death, just as we befriend others who also need our care. Holy Saturday is a day for resting in our humanity, as we give thanks for the community that surrounds us on every side. On this day we know we are mortal, and yet, in the words of the Holy Saturday collect, we rest on this day so that we "may await with him the coming of the third day, and rise with him to newness of life" (BCP 283).

QUESTIONS FOR FURTHER THOUGHT AND DISCUSSION

1. What are some of your most memorable moments during Holy Week in the past?

2. If you, like Egeria, were writing to a friend about Holy Week in the Episcopal Church today, how would you describe the events of this special week in your congregation?

3. If you have heard or participated in the reading of the passion gospel on Palm Sunday or Good Friday in previous years, how has it affected your understanding of the gospel? Why do you think the early church found it important to read the passion gospel over and over again in Holy Week?

4. If you have participated in the footwashing on Maundy Thursday in previous years, what was your experience like? If you have not, would you like to try it now? Why or why not?

5. One of the prayers you will hear often during Holy Week is the prayer that begins, "Almighty God, we pray you graciously to behold this your family. . . ." The entire text of the prayer can be found at the beginning of the Good Friday liturgy (BCP 276). As you read this prayer again, reflect on what it means to be a member of God's "family."

Easter to Pentecost

Almighty God, who through your only-begotten Son Jesus Christ
overcame death and opened to us the gate of everlasting life: Grant
that we, who celebrate with joy the day of the Lord's resurrection,
may be raised from the death of sin by your life-giving Spirit.

Collect for Easter Day (BCP 222)

Like Christmas, the other widely popular feast of the church, Easter has become a holiday that is celebrated in western American culture as well as in the church, though with rather different associations. If you are looking for an Easter card to send a friend or loved one, you will find an odd assortment of greetings, from "Happy Spring!" to a variety of religious sentiments. Most will be decorated with bunnies, baby birds, butterflies, or flowers in pastel colors. Catalogs will sell you "egg trees" for hanging decorated Easter eggs, and in the malls children can have their pictures taken with the Easter Bunny to put beside their photos with Santa. And families with young children almost always dye multicolored eggs for the Easter Bunny to hide on Easter morning.

These associations of Easter with spring are part of a parallel tradition of celebrating the time of year when the earth thaws and new growth appears, which in some parts of the world coincides with the time of year in which Christians celebrate new life in Jesus' resurrection. Just as Christmas was established as a Christian feast on the day of the Roman festival of the birth of their sun god, Easter likewise has connections to the religions of the surrounding cultures. The word "Easter" comes from *Eostre,* the name of a Teutonic goddess associated with the return of the season of growth and fertility at springtime.

The season of Easter also corresponded to the Hebrew Feast of Weeks, which began at Passover and ended on the fiftieth day as Shavuot or Pentecost. This was originally an agricultural feast, but later celebrated the giving of the law to Moses on Mount Sinai. In many countries the name of the Christian feast we call Easter is still called by its older Greek name, *Pascha,* which means "Passover," and it is this meaning as the Christian Passover—the celebration of Jesus' triumph over death and entrance into resurrected life—that is the heart of Easter in the church. For the early church, Jesus Christ was the fulfillment of the Jewish Passover feast: through Jesus, we have been freed from the slavery of sin and granted entry to the Promised Land of everlasting life.

Easter, the oldest celebration of the Christian year, is not a single day but an entire season: Easter lasts fifty days, from Easter Day (the Sunday of the Resurrection) through the Day of Pentecost. The season also includes the feast of the Ascension, when the resurrected Jesus ascended to heaven and was seen on earth no longer. Throughout the year every Sunday—even during Lent— is considered a little Easter, a mini feast of the resurrection on what Christians have called the first day of the week.

All the other seasons grew up around this most ancient feast. Lent, for example, developed as a time of preparation for Easter baptisms. Our churches tend to be filled with classes, forums, retreats, and activities during Lent, but after Easter the schedule of events slows down. In the early catechumenate, this season was a time called *mystagogia*—the learning of the "mysteries" of the faith, particularly baptism and Eucharist. And many congregations today are likewise making an effort to provide ongoing opportunities for continued prayer, learning, and formation in the Christian faith and life during the seven weeks of Easter.

EASTER THEMES

The primary theme of Easter is the resurrection: on this day Jesus was raised from the dead, overcoming the power of death and the grave. We celebrate that we, too, are raised to everlasting life with him in our baptism. The ancient traditional Easter greeting conveys this theme with joy and praise:

"Alleluia! Christ is risen!"
"The Lord is risen indeed! Alleluia!"

As often is the case, the hymns of the church for the Easter season provide a wealth of resources for celebrating and understanding this almost unbelievably good news. An ancient hymn by John of Damascus combines the imagery of Israel's exodus from Egypt with the breaking of the bonds of sin and death:

Come, ye faithful, raise the strain of triumphant gladness!
God hath brought his Israel into joy from sadness:
loosed from Pharoah's [*sic*] bitter yoke Jacob's sons and
   daughters,
led them with unmoistened foot through the Red Sea waters.

'Tis the spring of souls today: Christ hath burst his prison,
and from three days' sleep in death as a sun hath risen;
all the winter of our sins, long and dark, is flying
from his light, to whom we give laud and praise undying.[47]

In addition to the theme of Christ's resurrection, the popular Easter focus on new life in the springtime of the year has been incorporated into Christian tradition as well. In the spring we see flowers emerging from the barren ground, trees in bud, birds building nests in which to lay their eggs. A twentieth-century

Easter hymn links Christ's resurrection with the new life of the earth in spring:

> Forth he came at Easter, like the risen grain,
> he that for three days in the grave had lain,
> quick from the dead my risen Lord is seen:
> Love is come again like wheat that springeth green.[48]

The power of "nature's Easter" was brought home to me one year at our parish in Wisconsin. There the winters are cold, hard, and long, and the welcome warmth of spring comes late. That year the children decorated paper "eggs" with symbols of Holy Week and Easter. The woman who was coordinating the children's Good Friday service brought in a large leafless branch stuck in a bucket of wet sand for the children to hang their artwork on. After the Good Friday liturgy we left the branch in the cold, quiet parish hall. When we arrived at church early in the morning on Easter Day we were amazed and awed to discover the branch had flowered: it was a forsythia branch, and the paper eggs were fluttering in the sunlight now amid beautiful, fresh yellow buds. For all of us, it was an unexpected and unforgettable moment of understanding the resurrection in a deeper way.

Integrally connected to the Easter themes of resurrection and new life is the focus on baptism, since in the church "we are buried with Christ by Baptism into his death, and raised with him to newness of life" (BCP 292). As we have noted before, the Easter Vigil was the time for baptisms in the early church, and Lent was the period of forty days of preparation for this life-changing event. In the same way, following those baptisms, during the period of fifty days called *mystagogia* the newly baptized heard sermons from their bishops on the meaning of the sacraments and theology of the church, and experienced the fullness of their communion within the community of the faithful by participating in the Eucharist for the first time.

Finally, another important theme of the Easter season is the giving of the Holy Spirit at Pentecost, in fulfillment of Jesus' promise to his disciples:

> *It is to your advantage that I go away, for if I do not go away, the Advocate will not come to you; but if I go, I will send him to you. . . . When the Spirit of truth comes, he will guide you into all the truth.* (John 16:7, 13)

We will look at the gift of the Holy Spirit more fully when we discuss the Day of Pentecost later in this chapter.

EASTER TRADITIONS

The traditional color for Easter vestments and altar hangings is white for joy and celebration. Often you will also see gold, bright red, and other festive colors interwoven in the fabric. I remember serving once as the deacon at a cathedral that owned an elaborate set of gold-colored vestments made of such extraordinarily hefty fabric that by the conclusion of the Easter liturgy my shoulders literally ached from the weight of the dalmatic. But even small congregations can create vestments of lovely fabrics to suit the occasion: the vestments and hangings for Easter are simply the most festive linens a congregation has, and their color and ornateness matters less than their beauty and careful craftsmanship.

You will probably notice a new, large white candle prominently displayed near the altar at the Easter services. This is called the paschal candle, and symbolizes Christ's light in the darkness, the triumph of life over death. It is first lit from the "new fire" at the Easter Vigil, and is so large because originally it was never extinguished for the fifty days until Pentecost. Most of our churches today extinguish it during the week because of the risk of fire, but the paschal candle will be lit for every service through Pentecost, as well as for every baptism throughout the year.

Oddly enough, the tradition of decorating colored eggs at Easter as a symbol of the emergence of new life predates Christianity. Evidently decorated eggs were exchanged as gifts to celebrate the coming of spring in ancient Egypt and Persia, and the Babylonians likewise considered the egg a worthy symbol of fertility and new life. The Christians of this region in Mesopotamia were probably the first to connect the decorating of eggs with the feast of the resurrection of Christ, and by the Middle Ages the practice was so widespread that in some places Easter Day was called Egg Sunday. In parts of Europe, the eggs were dyed red and were then cracked together when people exchanged Easter greetings.[49] Many congregations today continue to have Easter egg hunts for the children after the services on Easter Day.

Another longstanding tradition at Easter time is feasting, after the long fast of Lent. Often we keep this tradition within our families only, but Easter is a good time to share a festive meal with other Christians as well. You might consider welcoming other members of your congregation to your Easter dinner this year.

THE EASTER VIGIL

The Easter Vigil is the first celebration of Easter, and is among the most ancient liturgies we have, dating at least to the second century if not earlier. Although the Vigil began to reappear in the Roman Catholic Church in the 1950s, it was only recently restored to our prayer book in the 1979 revision, so in some Episcopal churches today it is still a new service—one that is well worth exploring. The Easter Vigil takes place the night before Easter Day: in the early church it would have begun at sunset and continued through the night until sunrise. In churches today the Vigil usually starts in the evening—perhaps eight o'clock or as late as ten—and lasts only a couple of hours. Despite the late hour, the Vigil can be a wonderful service for older children because it is the epitome of "hands-on" liturgy, especially if they are serving as acolytes in the service. Children also love the contrasting symbols of light and darkness, quiet reflection and loud rejoicing.

There are four main parts to the Easter Vigil: the Service of Light, in which we light the new fire and the paschal candle; the Service of Lessons, in which we hear readings from Scripture;

Christian Initiation, in which we celebrate baptisms and the renewal of vows; and the Holy Eucharist, in which we partake of our Easter communion. At some point during Holy Week you may be asked to bring two unusual items to this service: a flashlight and a small bell.

The Service of Light

When you arrive at the darkened church for the Easter Vigil you will discover why you were asked to bring the flashlight. All of the candles and lights have been extinguished in anticipation of this event, and you may need the flashlight to find your seat. In ancient times the kindling of a flame for light meant serious effort, not the simple striking of a match. The extinguishing of light and the rekindling of fire became a powerful symbol of death and new life. So at the Easter Vigil we move from the darkness of Good Friday and Holy Saturday to the light of Easter morning.

Usually the new fire is started in a metal container (some churches use a charcoal grill) just outside the door of the church or in a safe location where the smoke will not pose a problem. After a prayer and perhaps the decorating of the paschal candle with symbols of Christ, the candle is lit from the new fire. The deacon or priest then carries the candle in procession into the dark church, pausing and singing "The light of Christ" three times.

At this point you may sense in a whole new way the power of a single light to dispel the darkness. We are so accustomed to having electricity readily available that we cannot always appreciate the significance of light. During a recent hurricane thousands of homes in our area lost power for several days, and although at first it was a novelty to light candles at night, after a few days my family began to dread the coming of evening. Candles took on a new importance: no longer simply an accent for a romantic dinner, they were our comfort in the shadows, a safeguard up and down stairways, a reminder of the hopeful light of day, a means for accomplishing tasks. They made it possible for us to see where we were going, and to carry on after sunset. A single candle can cast a large circle of light, and as we gather around its warmth we experience a new connection with the people around us. You may have been given small candles when you arrived at church this evening; these candles are now lit from the paschal candle. Take time to look around you: your familiar church probably looks different in candlelight. The faces of the people around you are transformed by the flickering lights in their hands. They are no longer strangers but fellow companions on the journey, all seeking refuge and comfort and strength and hope in the light of this church on this dark night.

After the deacon or priest places the paschal candle in its stand by the altar, he or she sings an ancient prayer called the *Exsultet.* This beautiful prayer by the paschal candle can be one of the most memorable moments of the service, if it is sung well (and memorable in other ways if not!). In any case, the words are well worth considering in your private prayer throughout the Easter season. They proclaim the meaning of Easter and call us to rejoice:

> *Rejoice now, heavenly hosts and choirs of angels,*
> *and let your trumpets shout Salvation*
> *for the victory of our mighty King.*
>
> *Rejoice and sing now, all the round earth,*
> *bright with a glorious splendor,*
> *for darkness has been vanquished by our eternal King.* (BCP 286)

A recurring phrase in the *Exsultet* is "This is the night," reminding us that, like the Jewish yearly celebration of Passover, Easter is not just the remembrance of Jesus' resurrection two thousand years ago, but the celebration of that resurrection experienced in our lives today, on *this* night:

> *This is the night, when you brought our fathers, the children of Israel, out of bondage in Egypt, and led them through the Red Sea on dry land.*

This is the night, when all who believe in Christ are delivered from the gloom of sin, and are restored to grace and holiness of life.

This is the night, when Christ broke the bonds of death and hell, and rose victorious from the grave. . . .

How blessed is this night, when earth and heaven are joined and man is reconciled to God. (BCP 287)

The Service of Lessons

At the heart of most vigils is the reading of a substantial number of Scripture passages, and this is certainly true of the Easter Vigil. After the singing of the *Exsultet* we hear in the readings from the Old Testament "the record of God's saving deeds in history, how he saved his people in ages past" (BCP 288). The number of lessons read may vary from two to nine, and include the stories of creation, Noah and the flood, Abraham's sacrifice of Isaac, and Israel's deliverance from slavery in Egypt at the Red Sea, as well as several important passages from the prophets about the hope of redemption and new life in the people of Israel.

After each reading there is a psalm and a prayer linking the reading with the Easter baptisms and celebration of new birth. This is the prayer after the passage from Genesis telling the story of Noah and the flood, for example:

Almighty God, you have placed in the skies the sign of your covenant with all living things: Grant that we, who are saved through water and the Spirit, may worthily offer to you our sacrifice of thanksgiving; through Jesus Christ our Lord. Amen. (BCP 289)

Christian Initiation

In the early church the Easter Vigil was the primary time for baptisms, and the baptism of new members remains central to the service today. Even if your congregation does not have a candidate for baptism at the Easter Vigil, the renewal of baptismal vows reminds us that baptism is the reason Easter has real meaning in our lives, for it is through our baptism that we are "raised with him to newness of life" (BCP 292). For those of us who were baptized as infants, the renewal of the vows made by our parents and godparents on our behalf is an important way to make these promises our own.

The Holy Eucharist

We have now come to a turning point in the service as we celebrate the first Eucharist of Easter. The candles on the altar are lit from the paschal candle, all hand-held candles are extinguished, and the electric lights are turned on. You may discover the altar space is surrounded by an abundance of Easter lilies and other flowers and greenery. The celebrant will proclaim the Easter greeting: "Alleluia. Christ is risen." "The Lord is risen indeed. Alleluia," the people respond. Suddenly the organ and perhaps a trumpet or two will break the silence. As you begin to sing the *Gloria in excelsis* for the first time in over forty days, you will know why you were asked to bring a bell—it is time to start ringing! Some congregations use tambourines and other hand-held instruments as well. This tradition is great fun for children of all ages. The joyful contrast to Lent is unmistakable, and as you blink in the light and sing the familiar song of praise you will no doubt see smiles of amazement on the faces around you. This is a moment when we glimpse a bit of heaven, and can believe again the Good News is indeed true after all.

EASTER DAY

This special Sunday is a day, like Christmas, when you will see a variety of longstanding local traditions at different parishes. Some have sunrise services rather than an Easter Vigil, to recall the experience of Mary Magdalene and "the other Mary" discovering the empty tomb "as the first day of the week was dawning" (Matthew 28:1). Others offer their normal schedule of Sunday services of the Eucharist but with festive music, perhaps baptisms, special treats at the coffee hour, and an egg hunt for the children.

If the Easter Vigil is the primary Easter service, these services on Easter Day can almost seem anticlimactic. Nevertheless, after the weeks of sober Lenten preparation and rigors of Holy Week, it is time to pull out all the stops, making "a joyful noise unto the Lord" and celebrating with the church throughout the ages and all creation this day of resurrection.

EASTER WEEK AND THE GREAT FIFTY DAYS

If Holy Week is one of the best-known weeks of the church year, Easter Week is certainly one of the least. In the early church the eight days after Easter (called the Easter octave, or Easter Week) were an important time for the newly baptized participants in the catechumenate to learn of the sacraments and "mysteries" of the church. We have largely lost this focus, and instead seem to need to catch up on other things after spending so much time in church. In most congregations, Easter Week is so quiet that the Sunday after Easter is even called "Low Sunday," because usually there is a lower than normal attendance at services that day.

The season of Easter, from Easter Day through the Day of Pentecost, is called the Great Fifty Days. As the 1979 Book of Common Prayer was being introduced, one of the contributors to the prayer book, Boone Porter, aptly remarked, "It is a strange irony that many church people try faithfully during Lent to observe forty days of preparation, yet virtually abandon Eastertide after going to church on Easter Day."[50] However, with the incorporation of the prayers and liturgies from the early church in our prayer book and the recovery of the catechumenate, Easter Week and the season of Easter are better known now than they were. You will find an increasing variety of opportunities to practice the faith you affirmed at the Easter Vigil, by sharing in prayer or Bible study groups, helping at soup kitchens, or joining the choir.

The prayer book provides Scripture readings and collects for each of the days of Easter Week that you can use at home in your daily devotions. Our *Lesser Feasts and Fasts* also offers lectionary propers and prayers for each of the weekdays of the Great Fifty Days of Easter, just as it does for Lent. And books are now available that contain excerpts of the sermons preached by bishops and teachers in the early church to the newly baptized.[51] The pilgrim Egeria wrote that the bishop in Jerusalem would deliver his sermons while seated in the door of the shrine built over Jesus' empty tomb. Reading these homilies from a chair in your home may seem rather mundane by comparison, but their message of the meaning of Easter is still timely in our own day.

The Sunday Liturgy in Easter

On the Sundays of the Great Fifty Days you will notice an abundance of "Alleluias" in the services, as well as the singing of glorious Easter hymns. The paschal candle remains lit for all of these services, through the Day of Pentecost, reminding us of the light of the resurrection. This is a time for reflecting on the meaning of our baptism and on the presence of the Holy Spirit in our lives and in the community we call the church. That makes it a time also to focus on the mission of the church as it seeks to live out its call to serve the world in Christ's name.

During the weeks of Easter we read passages from the Acts of the Apostles, the continuation of the gospel according to Luke that tells the story of the early days of the church. There we hear about how the first Christians spread the news of their experience of Jesus and their conviction that in Jesus God had brought about a new reign of love and mercy. Hearing their story helps the church today understand its mission to witness to its own experience of Christ in the Holy Spirit. In Acts we see men and women who were fearful, disappointed, and distraught on Good Friday transformed into leaders and evangelists filled with joyful assurance, teaching and healing as Jesus had done.

Every three years, during Year A of the lectionary, we hear readings from the first letter of Peter, which some scholars believe was part of an early baptismal rite of prayers and catechetical instruction. The letter speaks of their "new birth into a living hope through the resurrection of Jesus Christ from the dead" (1 Peter 1:3) and urges these new Christians to act in accordance with their baptismal promises:

> *As he who called you is holy, be holy yourselves in all your*
> *conduct. . . . You have been born anew . . . through the living*
> *and enduring word of God. . . . Rid yourselves, therefore, of all*
> *malice, and all guile, insincerity, envy, and all slander. Like*
> *newborn infants, long for the pure, spiritual milk, so that by it*
> *you may grow into salvation.* (1 Peter 1:15, 23, 2:1–2)

The gospel readings during these weeks tell of Jesus' appearances to the disciples. We hear of the request of "doubting Thomas" to see the wounds in Jesus' hands and side, of the dejected disciples returning to Emmaus after the Passover who recognized Jesus only as they broke bread together, and of Jesus' appearance to the seven disciples by the Sea of Tiberias, as he showed the fishermen where to find an enormous catch while he prepared breakfast for them on the shore. The gospel readings also recount Jesus' final words to his disciples concerning the community they would be establishing after his death and resurrection:

> *I give you a new commandment, that you love one another. Just*
> *as I have loved you, you also should love one another. By this*
> *everyone will know that you are my disciples, if you have love for*
> *one another.* (John 13:34–35)

> *I have said these things to you while I am still with you. But the*
> *Advocate, the Holy Spirit, whom the Father will send in my*
> *name, will teach you everything, and remind you of all that I*
> *have said to you. Peace I leave with you; my peace I give to you.*
> *I do not give to you as the world gives. Do not let your hearts be*
> *troubled, and do not let them be afraid.* (John 14:25–27)

THE ASCENSION

The feast of the Ascension suffers from the same affliction Epiphany does when it falls on a weekday, and so is missed by those who can attend church services only on Sunday. In Acts, Luke tells us Jesus appeared to the disciples "during forty days" and then ascended into heaven, so the feast of the Ascension is always on a Thursday. In many places you will find a special evening celebration of the Eucharist and perhaps a parish supper on Ascension Day, and these are well worth attending during this season of learning what it means to live together as a community of believers.

Luke tells the story of the ascension in both his gospel and in the Acts of the Apostles. After Jesus had taught his disciples and "opened their minds to understand the Scriptures," he blessed them.

> *While he was blessing them, he withdrew from them and was carried up into heaven. And they worshiped him, and returned to Jerusalem with great joy; and they were continually in the temple blessing God.* (Luke 24:51–53)

In Acts, Luke adds more detail to the story:

> *As they were watching, he was lifted up, and a cloud took him out of their sight. While he was going and they were gazing up toward heaven, suddenly two men in white robes stood by them. They said, "Men of Galilee, why do you stand looking up toward heaven? This Jesus, who has been taken up from you into heaven, will come in the same way as you saw him go into heaven."* (Acts 1:9–11)

Homilists will often ask the same question of us when we focus too much on "spiritual" things and neglect to care for the people beside us and for the earth with all its creatures.

The hymns for the Ascension likewise convey the meaning of this day: it is the completion of Jesus' work of redemption, as he takes his seat "at the right hand of the Father." But rather than trying to imagine an arrangement of heavenly thrones on puffs of clouds, we rejoice on this day that Christ has taken our human nature into heaven and from there intercedes for us at every moment.

Jesus' ascension is also an important moment in the formation of the church: without the ascension, the church would have remained dependent on the appearances of the resurrected Jesus. Instead of being transformed by the power of the Holy Spirit in their lives and enabled to move forward into the future, the disciples would have talked among themselves about the latest appearance and waited anxiously for another one. Such a church calls to mind some communities formed around the appearances of a certain saint or the Virgin Mary. If these appearances are not kept in perspective, they can stunt the growth of believers who sit and wait for yet another appearance rather than moving on with their lives and practicing their ministries in this world. Jesus tells his disciples repeatedly that it was a *good* thing for him to leave them:

> *Because I have said these things to you, sorrow has filled your hearts. Nevertheless I tell you the truth: it is to your advantage that I go away, for if I do not go away, the Advocate will not come to you; but if I go, I will send him to you.* (John 16:6–7)

In other words, we could not have had Pentecost without Jesus' ascension.

THE DAY OF PENTECOST

On this important feast day of the church we celebrate the outpouring of the Holy Spirit and the ongoing life of the Holy Spirit in the church today. The feast of Pentecost is the last day of the Easter season, and is celebrated ten days after the Ascension, fifty days after Easter—its name comes from the Greek, meaning "fiftieth day." Pentecost was also the Greek name for the Hebrew Feast of Weeks, the celebration of the giving of the law to Moses on Mount Sinai, which was kept on the fiftieth day after Passover. The disciples were gathered in Jerusalem to celebrate this Jewish Pentecost when the Holy Spirit was poured out on the disciples, transforming them into a vibrant, evangelizing community of believers. As the "birthday" of the church, the feast of Pentecost is among the most important and festive days in the church calendar.

The color for the altar hangings and vestments on Pentecost is red instead of Easter white, to symbolize the "tongues of fire" Luke uses to describe the descent of the Holy Spirit. You may also see people in the congregation wearing red clothing, as a fun way of keeping the feast—though ironically an older name for this day is Whitsunday, or "white Sunday," named for the white garments worn by the newly baptized. Another tradition is to hang red balloons in the parish hall, as in a birthday party. Some congregations have a traditional birthday cake for the coffee hour. One of the most beautiful symbols of Pentecost you will often see in the church today is a paper or fabric dove (symbolizing the Holy Spirit, who "descended like a dove" at Jesus' baptism) mounted like a kite on a long stick with streamers and carried in procession, soaring above the heads of those in the congregation.

The prayer book notes that Pentecost is one of the four days on which baptisms are most appropriately scheduled, since it is part of the Easter season. In the medieval church Pentecost became a sort of "make-up" day for those who missed being baptized on Easter Day. If your congregation does not have any candidates for baptism on Pentecost this year, everyone will renew their baptismal vows, as at the Easter Vigil, instead.

One custom that is becoming increasingly popular today is to have the gospel for this day read in at least two and perhaps several languages, to symbolize the many languages in which the gospel was heard on that first Christian Pentecost: "All of them were filled with the Holy Spirit and began to speak in other languages, as the Spirit gave them ability" (Acts 2:4). When I first heard this done I thought it was merely a way to use the liturgy to make a point about multiculturalism. Over time, however, I have found it to be an enriching dimension of the service, helping to expand my sense of the multitude of people and cultures who make up the church. Hearing the gospel in different languages has also deepened my understanding of what it is like to try to participate in a liturgy in a language you do not know, and I now look forward to hearing the gospel proclaimed in several languages each Pentecost.

We are so accustomed to hearing about the Holy Spirit it can be difficult for us to realize the significance of the gift of the Spirit in our lives. Until that first Christian Pentecost, the Spirit of God rested only on certain individuals—such as the prophets, or some of the righteous kings of Israel—and only for a limited time. The idea that the Spirit would be poured out so liberally and so continuously, that the Spirit of God would remain with us all, was a profound shift for the Jewish Christians who witnessed that astounding day in Jerusalem.

It is the Holy Spirit who breathes life into the Body of Christ, the church; it is the Holy Spirit who provides the gifts and guidance needed to sustain our life. At every Eucharist we pray that the Holy Spirit will sanctify the bread and wine of communion to be "the Body and Blood of your Son, the holy food and drink of new and unending life in him." We also pray that the Spirit will "sanctify us also" so that we may receive the Eucharist with faith and serve God "in unity, constancy, and peace" (BCP 363). It is the Holy Spirit who makes God present and alive in our hearts.

QUESTIONS FOR FURTHER THOUGHT AND DISCUSSION

1. What Easter traditions do you remember keeping as a child? What traditions have you chosen to pass on to your children and grandchildren? Why?

2. Christians have long kept Easter not merely as a celebration of Jesus' resurrection at a certain point in human history, but as a celebration of new life in the present moment. Where do you see glimpses of the power of God's life overcoming death in the world today? In your own life?

3. Read the *Exsultet,* found on pages 286 and 287 of The Book of Common Prayer. What Easter themes do you hear? How does this text affect your understanding of the meaning of Easter?

4. How do you understand Jesus' ascension?

5. In what ways do you perceive the Holy Spirit is alive and active in the church today? In the world? In your life?

The Season after Pentecost

Lord of all power and might, the author and giver of all good things: Graft in our hearts the love of your Name; increase in us true religion; nourish us with all goodness; and bring forth in us the fruit of good works.

Collect for Proper 17 (BCP 233)

The Season after Pentecost is not actually a season with a single common focus, but is simply the weeks between the Day of Pentecost and the First Sunday of Advent. In the Roman Catholic Church it is often called "Ordinary Time," and many Episcopalians have adopted this name as well. These weeks hold both the slower pace and peaceful quality of summer months and the quicker pace and flurry of activity in the early fall. These are our "ordinary" days, in which we live the Christian faith in our daily lives.

During these weeks, as the liturgical scholar Leonel Mitchell puts it, we celebrate "the time in which we actually live—the period between the Pentecost and the Second Advent."[52] Two thousand years after the first Pentecost, the church still lives in this "in between" time before the fulfillment of time in Christ's second coming. You might also hear these weeks called "the long, green season," referring both to the green color of the vestments and altar hangings for these weeks as well as to the summertime of year in which many of the weeks fall in the northern hemisphere. After Pentecost we settle into the growing season, nourishing the seeds planted at Easter and putting down roots in our faith.

The church calendar identifies the weeks of the Season after Pentecost by numbering them: each "proper"—the prayers and Scripture readings assigned for that week—is given a number. The first Sunday after Pentecost is Trinity Sunday, so Proper 1 is actually the second Sunday after Pentecost. The confusing part is that since Easter (and therefore Pentecost) is a moveable feast, the date on which the numbered propers begin will vary each year. So the propers for each week are also linked to the monthly calendar: Proper 1, for example, is for the "Week of the Sunday closest to May 11." When Easter is late in the spring, the Sundays after Pentecost may skip the first few propers and start with Proper 3 or 4. You need not worry about missing any propers, though: they are the same as those at the end of the Season after the Epiphany and you would have heard them then, before Lent. It is as if the seasons of Lent and Easter "slide" up and down the numbered propers, depending when the full moon sets the date for Easter that year.

TRINITY SUNDAY

On this first Sunday after Pentecost we celebrate the doctrine of the Trinity. The Catechism describes the Holy Spirit as "the Third Person of the Trinity, God at work in the world and in the Church even now" (BCP 852). Throughout Lent and Easter we have focused on the second person of the Trinity, Jesus Christ. So it makes perfect sense for the church now to turn its attention to the fullness of God as Father, Son, and Holy Spirit. Although today we have reduced the focus on the Trinity to a single Sunday, in the 1928 prayer book the weeks we call the Season after Pentecost were called the Trinity Season.

Theologically, the doctrine of the Trinity is described in complex philosophical terms that are translated into English from the original Latin, and are therefore carefully and subtly nuanced and interpreted. This distance and the use of technical terms thus make the doctrine of the Trinity rather difficult to comprehend without studied effort. (That is why seminarians and new clergy assistants often find themselves assigned to preach on this Sunday!) So it is important to remember that the doctrine did not just "arrive" whole and intact one day: rather, it emerged from the early church's struggle to describe their experience of Jesus and the Spirit.

The early Christians had discovered Jesus to be more than a great prophet, more than a wise teacher, more than a kind healer. After the resurrection and ascension they experienced him as somehow related to God, as somehow part of the Godhead, and they struggled to understand exactly how this could be. Jesus had spoken of God as his Father, and of himself as the Son. After Pentecost, they also knew the Holy Spirit as somehow residing within them, distinct from Jesus and God the Creator, and yet also part of God. Their Jewish tradition told them consistently and clearly that God was One, not two or three. So how could this be? What evolved was the doctrine of the Trinity, which attempted to summarize their experience of God, just as it describes our experience of God today.

The Creed of Saint Athanasius, composed by several church leaders around the fourth or fifth century, summarizes in detailed philosophical terms the church's development of the doctrine of the Trinity. (You can find this creed in the prayer book under Historical Documents.) The main point of the document is that God is a Unity—"they are not three Gods, but one God"—and yet God is three persons—"there is one Person of the Father, another of the Son, and another of the Holy Ghost. . . . So the Father is God, the Son is God, and the Holy Ghost is God" (BCP 864–65).

It is indeed a mystery as to how God can be one God, and yet three persons; but when we reflect on our own relationships we can begin to grasp intuitively how this might be. Experientially, we already know God as Trinity through our loving relationships with God, ourselves, and other people. The theologian Mark McIntosh speaks of the Trinity as part of this essential pattern of human relationships as well as of the relationship of the Father, Son, and Spirit within God:

> The patterns and movement of our common life are sacraments of something greater and deeper: that pattern of eternal loving, giving, and receiving that is the only fruitful ground of all our relationships. Our yearning for communion with beauty in all its many forms whispers to us of the Holy Spirit, who would draw us into Communion itself: the communion of Father, Son, and Holy Spirit that is God's own life.[53]

The doctrine of the Trinity tells us that God is not a "cosmic principle" but a communion of love among persons. When we reflect on the ways we experience this sense of union yet distinction within our closest relationships in our families, particularly the experience of loving union that leads to the creation of a separate being, a child, we may discover a similar pattern at work and thus begin to glimpse the life of the Trinity.

Gretchen Wolff Pritchard has made a helpful distinction to consider on Trinity Sunday as well. As we struggle to understand the "intellectual puzzle" of the doctrine of the Trinity, she suggests, we need to remember that in our worship the concept of the Trinity "serves rather to draw us into contemplation of *God's experience of God.*" Pritchard reminds us that God's life is a relationship of love, so that when we draw near to that life in worship, we, too, are drawn "ever more deeply into love."[54] On this Sunday of the church year we explore, however dimly and inadequately, the inner life of God and are thus drawn not only into the intellectually challenging mystery of who God is, but also into the loving communion of the persons of the Trinity.

Although the early church defined the Trinity in terms of the persons of the Father, the Son, and the Holy Spirit, you will also hear other names for God the Trinity used in the church today. God as Creator, Redeemer, and Sanctifier is a common parallel used by many to avoid the masculine images of Father and Son, though some argue that these are the *functions* of the Trinity rather than names signifying their relationship within the Trinity, so they should not be considered equivalent terms. They are nevertheless useful for offering insights into the many different facets of God.

The vestments and altar hangings for Trinity Sunday are white, and there are a number of symbols of the Trinity, such as three interlocking circles or triangles, signifying three in one, that can be woven into the fabric. The Trinity permeates the prayers and blessings of the church: watch for references to the Trinity in the coming weeks. You will notice that most of the prayers in the prayer book conclude with an ascription like "through Jesus Christ our Lord, who lives and reigns with you and the Holy Spirit, one God, now and for ever." Following Jesus' directive to his disciples in Matthew 28, we are baptized "in the Name of the Father, and of the Son, and of the Holy Spirit" (BCP 307). And at the end of most services you will receive a blessing in the name of the Trinity, as in this seasonal blessing for Trinity Sunday:

> May God the Holy Trinity make you strong in faith and love, defend you on every side, and guide you in truth and peace; and the blessing of God Almighty, the Father, the Son, and the Holy Spirit, be among you, and remain with you always. *Amen.* (*BOS* 28)

There are a number of hymns celebrating God as Trinity in our hymnal, and you will no doubt sing several of them on Trinity Sunday. One of the most powerfully moving and encouraging hymns of the church is "St. Patrick's Breastplate," often sung at ordinations, baptisms, confirmations, and on major feasts. Its final refrain is a wonderful expression of the doctrine of the Trinity at work in our lives:

> I bind unto myself the Name,
> the strong Name of the Trinity,

by invocation of the same,
the Three in One, and One in Three.
Of whom all nature hath creation,
eternal Father, Spirit, Word:
praise to the Lord of my salvation,
salvation is of Christ the Lord.[55]

THEMES IN THE SEASON AFTER PENTECOST

Each Sunday of these weeks has its own theme, based on the collect, the first reading from the Old Testament or the Acts of the Apostles, and the gospel reading. Like the gospel readings, the epistle readings are sequential during these weeks in order to hear all or most of an entire letter, but they do not always fit with the specific weekly theme set by the gospel. The educator Joseph Russell has identified four general themes you may recognize in the readings and sermons during these weeks:

- Our relationship with God;
- Our relationship with Jesus Christ and with one another through our prayers, the sacraments, and life in the body of Christ;
- The presence of the Holy Spirit in our lives;
- The church and its mission.[56]

It can be helpful to keep these overarching themes of relationship and mission in mind as you move through the weeks of Ordinary Time.

One of the gifts of this time in the Christian calendar is the opportunity to hear some of the books of the Bible read as a whole, rather than in small snippets. We hear large sections of the gospels during these weeks, as well as entire letters from the apostles to the early Christian communities. In Year A we hear portions of the gospel according to Matthew; in Year B we hear Mark, and in Year C, Luke. Reading the gospel passages in sequence gives us a sense of the rhythm of Jesus' years of ministry, as he lived and taught and healed the people who sought him out.

During these weeks we hear portions of the Sermon on the Mount and many of the parables Jesus used in his teaching:

The kingdom of heaven is like treasure hidden in a field, which someone found and hid; then in his joy he goes and sells all that he has and buys that field. (Matthew 13:44)

We also hear Jesus' teachings on prayer, possessions, relationships within the kingdom of God, and the practice of justice:

You have heard that it was said, "An eye for an eye and a tooth for a tooth." But I say to you, Do not resist an evildoer. But if anyone strikes you on the right cheek, turn the other also; and if anyone wants to sue you and take your coat, give your cloak as well; and if anyone forces you to go one mile, go also the second mile. Give to everyone who begs from you, and do not refuse anyone who wants to borrow from you. (Matthew 5:38–42)

We see him healing the sick and lame, the demon possessed and the dying:

They brought to him a deaf man who had an impediment in his speech; and they begged him to lay his hand on him. He took him aside in private, away from the crowd, and put his fingers into his ears, and he spat and touched his tongue. Then looking up to heaven, he sighed and said to him, "Ephphatha," that is, "Be opened." And immediately his ears were opened, his tongue was released, and he spoke plainly. . . . They were astounded beyond measure, saying, "He has done everything well; he even makes the deaf to hear and the mute to speak." (Mark 7:32–37)

And like the multitudes who gathered around Jesus, we are amazed by the miracles he wrought in the feeding of the five thousand and the stilling of the storm on the Sea of Galilee.

These weeks are also a time of learning what it means to be a follower of Jesus. We see him calling the twelve to go out "two by two," carrying nothing but a walking stick, sending them out with authority to heal the sick and call the people to repentance. All the while, we know that during these weeks after Pentecost we are walking with Jesus and his disciples toward Jerusalem. We listen to Jesus' words of sober warning concerning his impending suffering and death and the cost of becoming his disciple.

Like the gospel readings, the epistle readings follow sequentially during the Season after Pentecost. In Year A we read most of Romans and substantial portions of 1 Corinthians, Philippians, and 1 Thessalonians. In Year B we follow with 2 Corinthians, Ephesians, James, and the letter to the Hebrews. And in Year C we read portions of Galatians, Colossians, 1 and 2 Timothy, Philemon, and 2 Thessalonians. Thus in the course of three years we hear read aloud as a community the same letters that were read aloud to those earliest communities of Christians, urging them to love one another and to hold fast to their faith in the midst of hardship, doubt, and persecution.

As we nourish our faith through the study of Scripture and the prayers of the Eucharist, we grow in our relationship with God and with our fellow Christians, coming to appreciate in new ways the ongoing presence of the Holy Spirit in our lives. And as we put down roots deep into the rich soil of community life, we participate more fully in the church's mission to the serve the world in Christ's name.

HOLY DAYS

The Season after Pentecost, lasting for several months, includes a number of holy days. Several of them celebrate various apostles, such as Peter and Paul, James, Bartholomew, Matthew, Simon, Jude, and Andrew, while others commemorate later saints of the church, such as Francis of Assisi, Hilda of Whitby, Leo the Great, Bernard of Clairvaux, and Augustine of Hippo. In Anglo-Catholic parishes the feast of St. Mary the Virgin, the mother of Jesus, on August 15 and Holy Cross Day on September 14 are significant occasions for parish festivals and liturgies. Two other holy days that are of particular note in many parishes during the weeks after Pentecost are the feast of the Transfiguration in August and All Saints' Day in November.

The Transfiguration

The feast of the Transfiguration of Our Lord on August 6 commemorates one of several occasions at which Jesus' identity as the Son of God is revealed—which is why we also read the story of Jesus' transfiguration on the last Sunday after the Epiphany. At Jesus' birth the angels herald his arrival, and at his death angels comfort the grieving disciples. At his baptism the Spirit descends on Jesus and a voice from heaven affirms, "This is my Son, the Beloved, with whom I am well pleased" (Matthew 3:17). Now, as Jesus prays on a mountain with Peter, James, and John, Jesus is transfigured before them and they see him as he truly is, his clothes dazzling white, his face full of glory. They hear a heavenly voice say once again, "This is my Son, my Chosen; listen to him!" (Luke 9:35).

The transfiguration is thus an important moment in Jesus' life, a moment of affirmation of his Father's love that would give him the strength to follow the path to Jerusalem and to endure the suffering that lay before him. But it also offers a glimpse of what lies ahead for us. We have all known times in our lives when we suddenly see things in a new light, when we see to the heart of someone, in a sense. In one of his most well-known sermons, "The Weight of Glory," C. S. Lewis speaks of the transfiguring of our neighbors in the fullness of time. "There are no *ordinary* people. You have never talked to a mere mortal," he reminds us.

> It is a serious thing to live in a society of possible gods and goddesses, to remember that the dullest and most uninteresting person you can talk to may one day be a creature which, if you saw it now, you would be strongly tempted to worship.[57]

The feast of the Transfiguration reminds us that Jesus was not an ordinary man. It also calls us to remember that we and our fellow human beings are not ordinary people either, and one day we hope to see them as they truly are, radiating the glory of God.

All Saints' Day

I confess that All Saints' Day has long been my favorite day in the church calendar, made even more special after one of my sons was baptized on that day. It is a day for remembering our loved ones who have gone on before us; it is also a day for celebrating our fellow Christians in the pew beside us. On this day we rejoice in the communion of all the saints, here and now, from before time and forever.

Celebrated on November 1, All Saints' Day follows All Hallow's Eve (Halloween) and precedes All Soul's Day, now rather euphemistically called the Commemoration of All Faithful Departed. In the Middle Ages "saints" were defined more narrowly than in the New Testament, which uses the word to describe all those who believe in Christ and are baptized in his name, so All Souls' Day was developed as an extension of All Saints' Day. It was a feast day for the rest of us, so to speak, not just the Christians who are recognized as exemplary witnesses to the gospel. But as the church has recovered more of the early church's vocabulary, theology, and liturgies in recent decades, the feast of All Saints has become a day for celebrating the ongoing communion of all believers, both those living today on earth and in eternity's heaven.

All Saints' Day is one of the principal feasts listed in our prayer book, which means it may be celebrated on the closest Sunday in addition to the actual date of November 1. It is also one of the days identified as appropriate for baptisms, since it is a celebration of the unity of all Christians from all the ages. You will probably sing this glorious and well-known hymn on the Sunday on which your parish celebrates All Saints':

For all the saints, who from their labors rest,
who thee by faith before the world confessed,
thy Name, O Jesus, be for ever blessed.
  Alleluia, alleluia! . . .

O blest communion, fellowship divine!
We feebly struggle, they in glory shine;
yet all are one in thee, for all are thine.
  Alleluia, alleluia![58]

THE LAST SUNDAY AFTER PENTECOST

The Sunday before Advent is often called Christ the King Sunday because the readings speak of the kingdom of God, and the reign of Christ as king. It is a relatively recent feast for the church: Pope Pius XI added it to the Roman Catholic Church's calendar in 1925, as a way of affirming the sovereignty of Christ in the midst of a troubled world. As we know from human history, the image of king or sovereign is a "mixed bag": for some it conveys positive attributes of the ability to bring about justice and to encourage the well-being of those under the king's authority. For others, the image of king is spoiled by the abuse and exploitation practiced by unjust rulers and dictators throughout the ages, and the patriarchal tyranny of male domination. For this image of Christ as king to be helpful, therefore, it is important for us to understand the nature of Christ's kingship.

The readings for Proper 29, which is the last Sunday after Pentecost and the Sunday before Advent, attempt to describe the kind of king Christ is. In Year B, for example, we hear Pilate ask Jesus, "So you are a king?" And Jesus replies, "You say that I am a king. For this I was born, and for this I came into the world, to testify to the truth" (John 18:37). Thus Christ's kingship has to do with a call to witness to what is true about God and Jesus' mission. According to the epistle reading in Year C, his kingship is also eternal, and over all creation from before time:

He is the image of the invisible God, the firstborn of all creation;
for in him all things in heaven and on earth were created, things
visible and invisible, whether thrones or dominions or rulers or
powers—all things have been created through him and for him.
(Colossians 1:15–16)

The gospel for Year C describes Christ's kingdom as a place
of peace and harmony and goodness, in contrast to the terrible
suffering we know in this earthly life. When the man who was
crucified next to Jesus begged him to "remember me when you
come into your kingdom," Jesus replied, "Truly I tell you, today
you will be with me in Paradise" (Luke 23:42–43).

In the "night visions" of Daniel read in Year A, we hear of "one
like a human being coming with the clouds of heaven":

To him was given dominion
*   and glory and kingship,*
that all peoples, nations, and languages
*   should serve him.*
His dominion is an everlasting dominion
*   that shall not pass away,*
and his kingship is one
*   that shall never be destroyed.* (Daniel 7:14)

When Christians interpret this passage as referring to Jesus, we
understand that his kingdom is over all the earth, from all time
and forever, and one that can never be destroyed, even by death.

In another prophecy from the Old Testament, read in Year A,
the prophet Ezekiel describes God in ways that remind Christians
of Jesus' identity as the Good Shepherd:

I myself will be the shepherd of my sheep, and I will make them
lie down, says the Lord GOD. *I will seek the lost, and I will bring*
back the strayed, and I will bind up the injured, and I will
strengthen the weak, but the fat and the strong I will destroy. I
will feed them with justice. (Ezekiel 34:15–16)

Thus in the kingdom of Christ the shepherd we see a reign of nurturing compassion and justice for the weak and injured and lost, as well as accountability for those who have exploited and overpowered others.

The Sunday of Christ the King is a fitting conclusion to the Season after Pentecost. During these weeks we have reflected on the life and ministry of Jesus as he proclaimed "the kingdom of God has come near," and on this final Sunday before Advent we affirm that in Jesus God has indeed brought about a new creation in a kingdom of merciful love and forgiveness. This feast is also a fitting herald to the approach of Advent, in which we prepare once again to welcome the One who came among us as a baby in Mary's arms long ago in Bethlehem, who comes among us even now in the bread and wine of the Eucharist, and who will come again in glory at the end of the ages.

Questions for Further Thought and Discussion

1. What is the usual schedule of your days in the weeks the church sometimes calls "Ordinary Time"? How do you give expression to your faith during this time of the year?

2. How would you explain the doctrine of the Trinity to someone who is unfamiliar with it? What is the most difficult aspect of the Trinity for you to communicate? Why?

3. Reread the well-known passage from C. S. Lewis's sermon "The Weight of Glory" quoted above in the section on the Transfiguration. In what ways do his words change your view of the people with whom you live, work, worship, or simply meet on the street? How do you imagine you will interact differently with them now?

4. The image of Christ the king is one that conveys different associations for many people in the church. In what ways do the readings for that Sunday help us understand this complex image? What helpful meanings does the image convey for you?

Notes

1. The Book of Common Prayer (New York: Church Hymnal, 1979), 15–33. (Hereafter BCP in text.)

2. Inos Biffi, *An Introduction to the Liturgical Year* (Grand Rapids: Eerdmans, 1994), 8.

3. Marianne H. Micks, *The Future Present: The Phenomenon of Christian Worship* (New York: Seabury Press, 1970), 45.

4. Micks, *Future Present,* 46–47.

5. Micks, *Future Present,* 47.

6. Massey Shepherd, Jr., *Liturgy and Education* (New York: Seabury Press, 1965), 98.

7. St. John Chrysostom, as quoted in *The Study of Liturgy,* ed. Cheslyn Jones, Geoffrey Wainwright, and Edward Yarnold, S.J. (New York: Oxford University Press, 1978), 405.

8. Joseph P. Russell, ed., *The New Prayer Book Guide to Christian Education,* rev. ed. (Cambridge, MA: Cowley Publications, 1996), xii.

9. Marion J. Hatchett, *Commentary on the American Prayer Book* (New York: Seabury Press, 1981), 38.

10. Hatchett, *Commentary,* 324–26.

11. H. Boone Porter, *Keeping the Church Year* (New York: Seabury Press, 1977), 31.

12. *The Book of Occasional Services* 2003 (New York: Church Publishing, 2004). (Hereafter *BOS* in text.)

13. Patricia B. Buckland, *Advent to Pentecost: A History of the Church Year* (Wilton, Conn.: Morehouse-Barlow, 1979), 29.

14. The Hymnal 1982 (New York: Church Hymnal, 1982), hymn 56.

15. Hymnal 1982, hymn 67. Words by Johann G. Olearius (1611–1684).

16. Porter, *Keeping the Church Year,* 10.

17. Josef A. Jungmann, S.J., *The Early Liturgy: To the Time of Gregory the Great,* trans. Francis A. Brunner, C.SS.R. (Notre Dame, Ind.: University of Notre Dame Press, 1959), 147–48.

18. J. Robert Wright, *Readings for the Daily Office from the Early Church* (New York: Church Hymnal, 1991), 41.

19. Hymnal 1982, hymn 82. Words by Marcus Aurelius Clemens Prudentius (348–410?).

20. Hymnal 1982, hymn 111. Words by Joseph Mohr (1792–1848).

21. Roland H. Bainton, ed., *Martin Luther's Christmas Book* (Minneapolis: Augsburg, 1948), 5.

22. Joseph P. Russell, *Sharing Our Biblical Story: A Guide to Using Liturgical Readings as the Core of Church and Family Education* (Minneapolis: Winston Press, 1979), 148.

23. Hymnal 1982, hymn 78. Words by Philips Brooks (1835–93).

24. The eastern churches are Orthodox churches (mainly in eastern Europe) that acknowledge the primacy of the Patriarch of Constantinople; the western churches are those who were under the authority of the Pope in Rome until the Reformation, as well as Protestant denominations that have emerged since that time. The Episcopal Church would be considered among the western churches.

25. Russell, *Sharing Our Biblical Story,* 146.

26. Russell, *New Prayer Book Guide,* 31.

27. Hymnal 1982, hymn 125. Words by John Morison (1749–98).

28. Hatchett, *Commentary,* 39.

29. Russell, *New Prayer Book Guide,* 31.

30. Wright, *Readings for the Daily Office,* 133.

31. Leonel L. Mitchell, *Lent, Holy Week, Easter, and the Great Fifty Days: A Ceremonial Guide* (Cambridge, MA: Cowley Publications, 1996), 3.

32. Dom Gregory Dix, *The Shape of the Liturgy* (London and New York: Continuum, 1945), 356.

33. Russell, *New Prayer Book Guide*, 65.

34. Hatchett, *Commentary*, 155–56.

35. Russell, *New Prayer Book Guide*, 63.

36. Russell, *New Prayer Book Guide*, 69.

37. *Lesser Feasts and Fasts* (New York: Church Hymnal, 1995), 58.

38. Russell, *New Prayer Book Guide*, 89–90.

39. Wright, *Readings for the Daily Office*, 165–66.

40. Wright, *Readings for the Daily Office*, 172–74.

41. Micks, *Future Present*, 45.

42. Dix, *Shape of the Liturgy*, 353.

43. Dix, *Shape of the Liturgy*, 225. See the rubric on BCP 270.

44. Hymnal 1982, hymn 154. Words by Theodulph of Orleans (d. 821).

45. Hymnal 1982, hymn 157.

46. Wright, *Readings for the Daily Office*, 172.

47. Hymnal 1982, hymn 200. Words by John of Damascus (8th century).

48. Hymnal 1982, hymn 204. Words by John Macleod Campbell Crum (1872–1958).

49. Buckland, *Advent to Pentecost*, 76.

50. Porter, *Keeping the Church Year*, 67.

51. See, for example, J. Robert Wright's *Readings for the Daily Office from the Early Church* (New York: Church Hymnal, 1991).

52. Mitchell, *Lent, Holy Week, Easter*, 121.

53. Mark McIntosh, *Mysteries of Faith*, vol. 8 of The New Church's Teaching Series (Cambridge, MA: Cowley Publications, 2000), 29.

54. Gretchen Wolff Pritchard, "The Sunday Paper" for Trinity Sunday (New Haven, Conn.: The Sunday Paper, 1988).

55. Hymnal 1982, hymn 370. Words attributed to St. Patrick (372–466).

56. Russell, *New Prayer Book Guide*, 125.

57. C. S. Lewis, *The Weight of Glory and Other Addresses* (San Francisco: HarperSanFrancisco, 1949 and 2001), 45–46.

58. Hymnal 1982, hymn 287. Words by William Walsham How (1823–97).